Plumbing Venting
Decoding Chapter 9 of the IPC

Bob Scott

ISBN-10: 0615904785
ISBN-13: 978-0-615-90478-8

DEDICATION

Dedicated to the Professionals who make our plumbing systems safe and reliable

CONTENTS

ACKNOWLEDGMENTS

I want to thank L. Fred Grable, PE with the International Code Council ® (ICC) for his help and guidance on understanding the intent and application of the International Plumbing Code (IPC). I also would like to thank and acknowledge the staff and management at the State of Colorado Plumbing Inspection Department for their many years of support, the Colorado Examining Board of Plumbers, my fellow state inspectors, the plumbing professionals, inspectors, designers and installers that I have interacted with over the years who teach *me* on a daily basis. Also, a big thanks to Justin Clark and his team at BIMSHIFT for their help in creating the CAD diagrams. Lastly, I would like to thank my beautiful and wonderful wife, Diane. Her support was the motivation to strive forward with the effort to create this illustrated guide.

FORWARD

I began my interest in writing a handbook to the plumbing code back in 2004. I was working for the State of Colorado Examining Board of Plumbers in the Denver office and was charged at the time with helping transition the state plumbers license exam from the existing adopted code of the Uniform Plumbing Code (UPC) to the current adopted code of the International Plumbing Code (IPC). Initially, I was asked to find the information that was the same in both codes for a "transitional" exam that would last approximately 6 months before the exam was wholly based on the IPC. This was a welcome challenge and in essence began what would eventually become my expertise, plumbing questions and the correct answers based on the relevant code section in the IPC. One of the big differences at the time between the two codes was the venting methods. Chapter 9 of the IPC offered more choices than the UPC. With more choices came more to learn and understand. Which systems could be used where…and what were the rules for each system (sizing, limitations, applicability etc.). Obviously, when developing state plumbing exams, they have to be accurate. So there was considerable time spent to understand these systems and the rules associated with them inside and out. I was lucky to be able to work with different Colorado plumbing license exam writing groups of plumbing professionals, plumbers and inspectors who were very knowledgeable and experienced on the code. With code cycles, a new edition was out every 3 years, so we would all re-group in our committees and start all over again preparing new test questions for the state exam every 3rd year. This experience has lent me a unique opportunity to learn the code very well and placed me in a position to share what I know with others. One of the things that became a powerful learning tool for me was seeing the venting systems in diagrams and also seeing them installed on construction projects. They say, "A picture is worth a thousand words". That is why I have developed this venting handbook with dozens of CAD drawings and field photographs to illustrate the many venting methods afforded by the 2015 IPC. There are many references to the 2015 IPC, and this manual is intended to be a handbook to the IPC code. It is helpful to have copy of the IPC code and the IPC commentary when using this manual. This book is not intended to be completely comprehensive to cover all aspects of plumbing venting but primarily to concentrate on the different venting methods available in the 2015 IPC. My hope is that the plumbing professional finds this illustrated book helpful and educational.

About the International Code Council

The International Code Council is a member-focused association. It is dedicated to developing model codes and standards used in the design, build and compliance process to construct safe, sustainable, affordable and resilient structures. Most U.S. communities and many global markets choose the International Codes. ICC Evaluation Service (ICC-ES) is the industry leader in performing technical evaluations for code compliance fostering safe and sustainable design and construction.

Headquarters: 500 New Jersey Avenue, NW, 6th Floor, Washington, DC 20001-2070

Regional Offices: Eastern Regional Office (BIR);

Central Regional Office (CH);

Western Regional Office (LA)

Phone: 888-ICC-SAFE (888-422-7233)

Website: www.iccsafe.org

1 VENTING DEFINITIONS

When determining how to choose which venting system to use and where, it is helpful to know the definitions specific to the terms used in the "Code". When you see the use the of the word "Code" in this manual, we are referencing the "International Plumbing Code (IPC), 2015 edition". When you see a word in italic in the Code, that word's definition is specific to the Code. That means the definition specific to the code may be different than you may find in a standard dictionary. The below definitions are some venting definitions from Chapter 2 of the Code, verbatim. They are listed here for your reference and convenience.

- **AAV-Air Admittance Valve** "One-way valve designed to allow air to enter the plumbing drainage system when negative pressures develop in the piping system. The device shall close by gravity and seal the vent terminal at zero differential pressure (no flow conditions) and under positive internal pressures. The purpose of an air admittance valve is to provide a method of allowing air to enter the plumbing drainage system without the use of a vent extended to open air and to prevent sewer gases from escaping into a building".

- **Bathroom Group** "A group of fixtures consisting of a water closet, lavatory, bathtub or shower, including or excluding a bidet, an *emergency floor drain* or both. Such fixtures are located together on the same floor level".

- **Branch** "Any part of the piping system except a riser, main or *stack*"

- **Branch Vent** "A vent connecting one or more individual vents with a vent *stack* or *stack* vent"

- **Circuit Vent** "A vent that connects to a horizontal drainage *branch* and vents two traps to a maximum of eight traps or trapped fixtures connected into a battery"

- **Combination Waste and Vent** "A specially designed system of waste piping embodying the horizontal wet venting of one or more sinks, lavatories, drinking fountains or floor drains by means of a common waste and vent pipe adequately sized to provide free movement of air above the flow line of the drain"

- **Common Vent** "A vent connecting at the junction of two fixture drains or to a fixture *branch* and serving as a vent for both fixtures"

- **Individual Vent,** "A pipe installed to vent a fixture trap and that connects with the vent system above the fixture served or terminates in the open air"

- **Relief Vent** "A vent whose primary function is to provide circulation of air between drainage and vent systems"

- **Stack** "A general term for any vertical line of soil, waste, vent or inside conductor piping that extends through at least one story with or without offsets"

- **Stack Vent** "The extension of a soil or waste *stack* above the highest horizontal drain connected to the *stack*"

- **Vent Stack** "A vertical vent pipe installed primarily for the purpose of providing circulation of air to and from any part of the drainage system"

VENTING DEFINITIONS cont.

Here are a few definitions that are not in chapter 2 of the Code. Some of the definitions listed below use the Code language from its respective section enhanced with a few of my own words.

• **Double Pattern Fitting** "A double wye or double combo fitting used in drainage and vent systems to connect back to back or side by side fixtures or branch drains. Double pattern fittings have a longer radius than similar fittings such as double fixture fittings or double sanitary tees"

• **Horizontal Wet Vent** "A horizontal vent system using any combination of fixtures within two bathroom groups located on the same floor level. The horizontal wet vent begins at the connection of the required dry vent connection and extends downstream to the last horizontally connected wet vented fixture drain. Each wet vented fixture drain connected shall connect independently and horizontally to the horizontal wet vent. The horizontal wet vent may not have vertical offsets. The required dry vent shall be an individual or common vent for any bathroom group fixture except for an emergency floor drain. Not more than one fixture may connect upstream from the dry vent connection to the horizontal wet vent"

• **Island Vent,** "A venting system permitted only for sinks and lavatories, residential kitchen sinks with or without a dishwasher, food grinder or both in combination with the kitchen sink waste. The vent connection to the waste shall rise to above the drainage outlet of the fixture before offsetting and returning downward to connect downstream of the fixture waste to the fixture branch drain. A foot vent shall connect on the vertical portion of the return vent near the connection to the fixture drain or immediately downstream and is permitted to run horizontally to a point where it shall run vertical to connect to either a vent stack, stack vent or to outside air. The horizontal vent piping shall be graded back to the drainage pipe by gravity. All vent offsets and drain connections shall be made with drainage fittings"

• **Single Stack Vent** "A drainage stack and its branches may serve as the vent for all of the fixtures discharging to the stack and its branches when sized to table 917.2 and installed to section 917 of the Code. The single stack shall remain vertical with no offsets between the lowest fixture drain or fixture branch and the highest fixture drain or branch connections <u>except</u> where the offset is vented in accordance with sections 907 and 917.7 of the Code. The stack vent must remain full size to termination. The horizontal branches connected to the single stack may be vented by the single stack itself in accordance with the limitations of section 917 of the code and/or the horizontal branches and its fixtures connected thereto must be vented in accordance with one of the methods in chapter 9 of the code. The type of fixture connected is not restricted"

• **Trap Weir** "The point on a trap where the water from the trap seal begins to flow down the fixture drain"

• **Waste Stack Vent** "A waste stack shall be considered the vent for all of the fixtures discharging to the stack when sized to Table 913.4 and installed to section 913 of the Code. Only fixture drains may connect to the stack. The waste stack shall remain vertical with no offsets between fixture drain connections. Offsets are only permitted below the lowest fixture drain connection or at least 6 inches above the flood rim of the highest fixture connected. The stack vent must remain full size to termination. Water Closets and Urinals are not permitted"

• **Wet-Vent** "A pipe that serves as both the drain *and* the vent for either a fixture or a group of fixtures"

• **Vertical Wet Vent** "A vertical vent system using any combination of fixtures within two bathroom groups located on the same floor level. The vertical wet vent begins at the connection of the required dry vent connection and extends downstream to the lowest fixture drain connection. Each wet vented fixture drain shall connect independently to the vertical wet vent. Water closets shall connect at the same elevation and shall be the lowest fixtures on the vertical wet vent. Other fixtures drains shall connect above or at the same elevation as the water closets. The required dry vent shall be an individual or common vent"

2 GENERAL REQUIREMENTS

As I mentioned in the forward, this handbook is focused on the different methods of venting provided for in Chapter 9 of the 2015 International Plumbing Code (IPC). Anytime I mention the word the "Code" in this handbook, I am referencing the 2015 IPC. Although this document is focused on the different methods of venting, it would be prudent to mention some of the general practices and venting requirements of the Code.

The primary function of a vent is to protect trap seals or in other words to prevent the trap of a fixture from siphoning and losing the water seal. The water seal is what prevents sewer gas from entering the building.

Section 706.3 of the Code: Fittings for change of direction. Fittings for change of direction can be found in table 706.3 of the Code. Although this table covers most of the fittings used in Drain, Waste and Vent (DWV), it will be helpful to illustrate a few of these fittings commonly used for DWV and the appropriate placement of them in relation to Venting. Watch for the proper placement of these fittings throughout this manual.

1. Sanitary Tees. This fitting may be used in several different positions for venting. In figure 1 below, the sanitary tee or "Santee" is in the vertical position. Here the vent would connect to the top of the fitting for an individual vent or when stacked with another tee, a common vent-connection at different levels. The configuration of a Santee allows the vent to connect above the weir of the trap as required in 909.2 of the Code (**Photograph 4**).

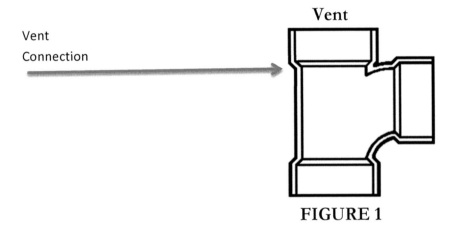

Vent

Vent
Connection

FIGURE 1

In figure 2, the Santee is located on its back. The dry-vent would connect to the "tee" side for an individual vent or a common vent. The arrow illustrates the flow of waste from the fixture or fixtures. A fixture may not drain into the vent of a Santee in the position shown in figure 2 as the Santee is not a drainage fitting in this position (706.3 of the Code).

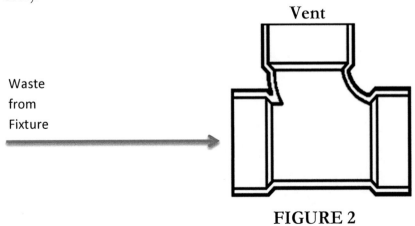

Vent

Waste
from
Fixture

FIGURE 2

The Santee fitting may dry vent a fixture in the position shown in both figures 1 & 2 with the vent connection positioned vertical to 45 degrees from the vertical and the vent pipe remaining vertical to a minimum of 6 inches above the highest flood rim before offsetting or connecting with another vent (Section 905.4 of the Code).

In figure 3, the Santee is upside down for a vent connecting a branch vent and an individual vent. The "Vent out" is where the vent would terminate to an approved location. The height of this tee must be a minimum of 6 inches above the highest flood rim of the fixtures connected. The Santee could also be located on its side and serve the same purpose for venting, but may not be positioned on its side (**Photograph 1**) for drainage.

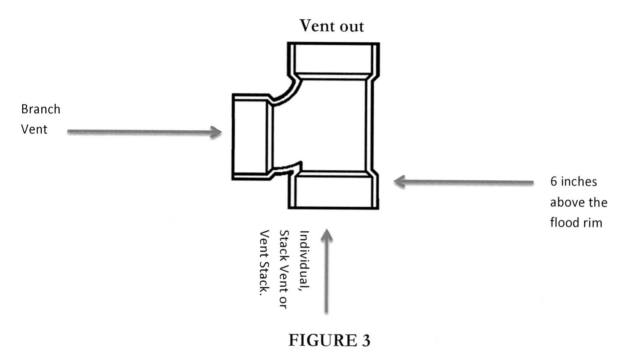

FIGURE 3

Note that in all of the diagrams the fittings are positioned in relation to direction of flow. In other words, if you were to dump water down the "vent out" it would drain back to the drainage pipe by gravity. In figure 4, the Santee is again used for connecting several vents together in the horizontal position.

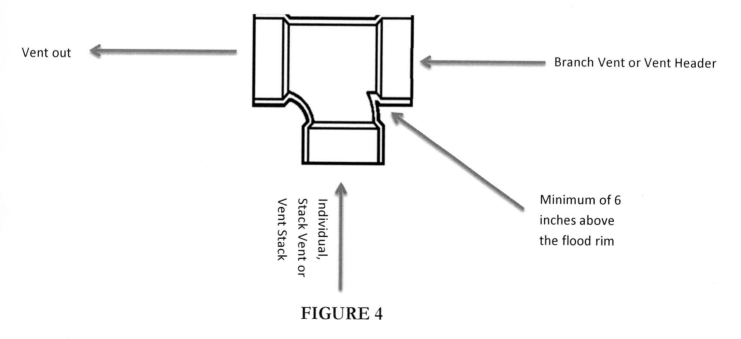

FIGURE 4

2. Double Sanitary Tees. See figure 5. These fittings are appropriate for use for back-to-back or side-by-side fixture drainage (common vents-connection at the same level) when used in the vertical position shown. The configuration of a Santee allows the vent to connect above the weir of the trap as required in 909.2 of the Code. When using this fitting to vent back-to-back water closets, it is important to remember that Section 706.3 has an "exception" to the Code that requires the horizontal developed length of the fixture drain from the water closet to be a minimum of 18 inches. The exception also states that double sanitary tee fittings shall **not** receive the discharge of fixtures or appliances of pumping action discharge. Examples are dishwashers or clothes washers.

This fitting is not proper for use on its side for drainage, but may be used upside down or on it's side for venting when positioned in the direction of flow connecting multiple vents located a minimum of 6 inches above the highest fixture served.

Vent

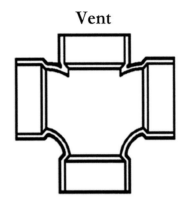

FIGURE 5

3. Double Fixture Fittings. Figure 6. This fitting is similar to a double sanitary tee and is appropriate for use for back-to-back or side-by-side fixture drainage when used in the vertical position shown. The configuration of a double fixture fitting allows the vent to connect above the weir of the trap as required by 909.2 of the Code.

With this fitting however, there are not the same limitations from section 706.3 with regard to pumping discharge or water closets that there are with double sanitary tees. Double fixture fittings are not appropriate for use on its side for drainage, but may be used on its side or upside down for venting when positioned in the direction of flow connecting multiple vents located a minimum of 6 inches above the highest fixture served.

Vent

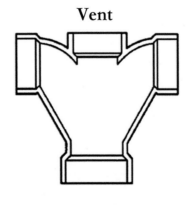

FIGURE 6

4. Combination Wye and 1/8 bend or "Combo" Figure 7. Combos are **not** proper for dry venting of a fixture in the vertical position as shown in figure 7. The vent connection is below the weir of a trap and prohibited by section 909.2 of the Code. This type of connection could cause siphonage of the fixture trap. The exception would be for a water closet or similar where the fixture is considered a "self-siphoning" fixture. Combos are appropriate for drainage in a vertical or a horizontal position (on its side) or on its back. Combos can also be used for venting when upside down, on its side or on its back when positioned in the direction of flow connecting multiple vents located a minimum of 6 inches above the highest fixture served.

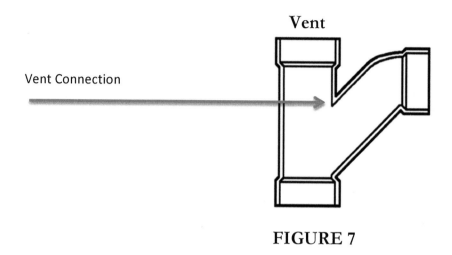

FIGURE 7

Combos are acceptable for venting (dry or wet) of a fixture when on its back (figure 8) and also on its side for wet venting. The combo fitting may dry vent a fixture in the position shown in figure 8 with the vent positioned vertical to 45 degrees from the vertical and the vent pipe remaining vertical to a minimum of 6 inches above the highest flood rim before offsetting or connecting with another vent.

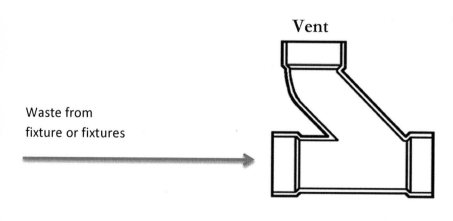

FIGURE 8

5. Double Pattern Fittings. Double Pattern Fittings are a common way to pick up back-to-back or side-by-side fixtures or drains in **wet-venting systems**. The proper choice and placement of these fittings is important in order to meet the code requirements. Double pattern fittings are not to be confused with double fixture fittings or double sanitary tees and should **not** be used in the vertical position as shown in figures 9 and 10 to dry vent back to back or side by side fixtures. Similar to the Combo shown in Figure 7, a Double Pattern Fitting has a vent connection below the weir of a trap and could cause siphonage of a fixture trap if used in this position. The exception would be for a water closet or similar fixture where the fixture is considered "self-siphoning". Figures 9 and 10 below illustrate Double Pattern Fittings.

Double Combination wye and 1/8 bend or "Double Combo" Figure 9. This wye and 1/8 bend or "Double Combo" can be used in the horizontal position to pick up back to back fixtures in many wet-venting systems such as circuit venting, horizontal common venting, horizontal wet-venting or combination waste and vent systems.

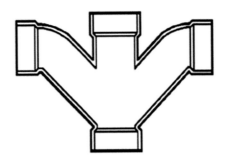

FIGURE 9
DOUBLE COMBO

Double Wye Figure 10. This Double Wye fitting us similar to the double combo and can be used in the horizontal position alone or with 1/8 bends to pick up back to back fixtures in many wet-venting systems such as circuit venting, horizontal common venting, horizontal wet-venting or combination waste and vent systems.

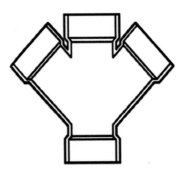

FIGURE 10
DOUBLE WYE

In this circuit vented sink configuration **(Photograph 1)** the sink downstream was piped with a Santee on its side for drainage. Table 706.3 of the Code does not permit the Santee in this position for drainage.

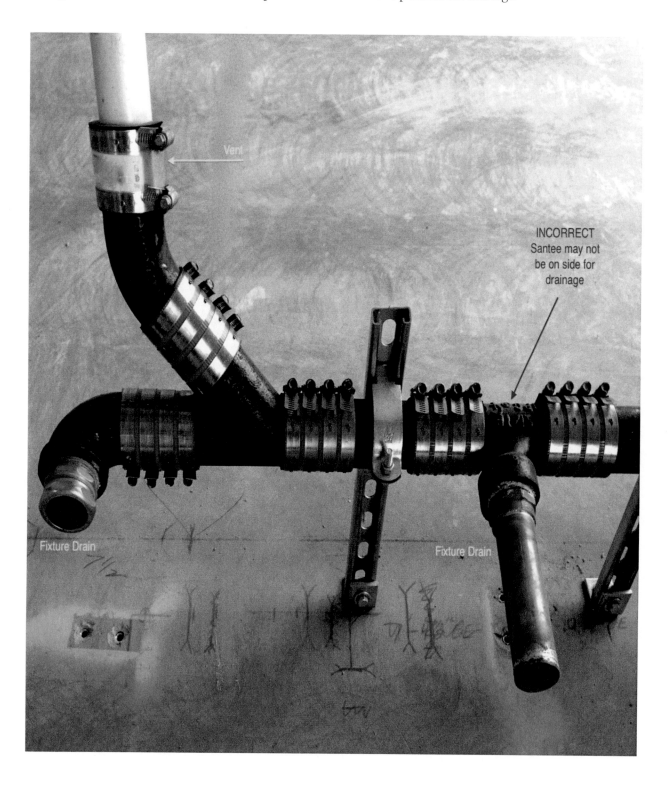

Photograph 1

Photograph 2 below shows an incorrect dry vent connection where a wye and 1/8 bend was used in the vertical position to vent a fixture drain. The vent connection is below the weir of the trap, which may cause the trap to siphon and is prohibited by section 909.2 of the Code.

Photograph 2

Photograph 3 shows a similar installation as Photograph 2, but with a Combo installed in the vertical position to vent the fixture. This long pattern fitting is not accepted for venting in this position as the trap weir is above the vent connection, which increases the possibility of siphonage and loss of trap seal.

Photograph 3

Photograph 4 below shows a properly vented fixture using a Santee. A Santee allows the vent connection above the weir of the trap which protects the trap seal from possible siphonage.

TRAP WEIR →

VENT CONNECTION
ABOVE TRAP WEIR

CORRECT VENT
CONNECTION

Photograph 4

Photograph 5 below is an example of a double fixture fitting (figure 6) used upside down to connect individual vents to a branch vent. Although this fitting was not specifically manufactured for this use, it is still an acceptable means to connect the vents.

Photograph 5

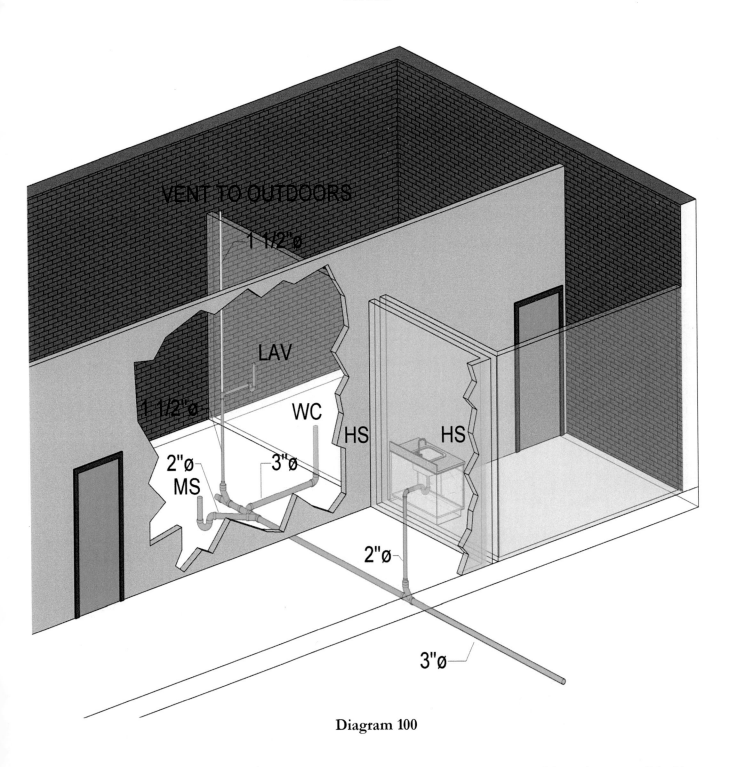

Diagram 100

Section 904.1 of the Code Each *building drain* must have at least one vent to the outdoors. This can be accomplished by a properly sized vent through the roof or through a sidewall (section 903.6). For example: You have a small detached retail store building **(Diagram 100)** where there is a sanitary building drain serving 1 hand sink, a mop sink and a unisex bathroom. The hand sink in this example is vented by a combination waste and vent pipe. On the other side of the building is the bathroom and janitor closet that has one vent serving the lavatory, floor drain, mop sink and toilet. The mop sink is vented by a combination waste and vent pipe. The water closet is vented by a horizontal wet vent from the lavatory. The lavatory vent would have to terminate outdoors. At least one vent serving a building drain shall terminate outdoors.

Section 901.2.1 of the Code-Venting required. "Traps and trapped fixtures shall (mandatory term) be vented in accordance with one of the venting methods specified in this chapter" (chapter 9) All the systems in Chapter 9 of the IPC are based on providing enough air so that the fixtures will drain properly and the trap seals will be protected. The theory is based on strict criteria for each venting method that provides for the "admission or emission of air so that the seal of any fixture trap shall not be subjected to a pressure differential of more than 1 inch water column". Basically, the wet venting methods we are covering are "oversized" to accommodate this pressure differential. These systems either must have not less than one vent to the outdoors or be connected to a building drain that has a vent that extends to the outdoors as stated in section 904.1 of the Code. So the Code language does state that it doesn't matter what the type of installation, a vent is always required when designing or installing a drainage system for plumbing fixtures. It may be a vent some distance from the actual trap or even a venting system. But in any case, a method of venting must always be provided for.

Section 905.3 and 905.4 of the Code - Vent connections and vertical rise. It is important to note the differences between "wet" and "dry" vents and the limitations for each. Vent connections that are "dry" must connect above the centerline of the of the horizontal pipe and may not offset horizontally until the vent has risen to at least 6 inches above the flood rim of the highest fixture connected. A "dry vent" is a vent that connects to a fixture drain and does not receive the discharge of any wastes. Its purpose is to provide air to protect the trap seal of the fixture or fixtures served. The dry vent must rise vertically (straight up to a max of 45 degrees from vertical) before offsetting or connecting to another vent.

Section 906 of the Code-Vent Pipe Sizing. When it comes to sizing your vents or vent systems, there are different methods to use based on what you are sizing. You will want to determine the type of vent or vent system and then simply use the correct methods.

With wet-vented systems, you will first need to know the size of the wet-vented piping. Remember the "wet-vented" piping is the piping serving as the drain *and* the vent. Common Vents with connections at different levels, Horizontal and Vertical Wet Vents, Waste Stack Vents, Combination Waste and Vent Systems and Single Stack Vent Systems all have sizing charts in their respective sections. Use these charts to size the wet-vented part of the system. With Circuit Venting, the wet-vented section is sized on the total fixture units discharged into the horizontal branch as determined in Table 709.1 and Tables 710.1 or 710.1(2).

To determine the vent sizing for the vent *serving* the wet-vent system, other methods are used. With Waste Stack Vents and Single Stack Vents, the *stack vent* serving these systems shall be the same size as the drainage stack. If a 4 inch Waste Stack is required by the fixture units as determined in Table 913.4, then the Waste Stack requires a 4-inch *stack vent* to termination. The same rule applies to Single Stack vent systems. If the size of the Single Stack is determined to be 6 inch according to Table 917.2, then the size of the stack vent serving that system shall be 6 inch.

For a single vent pipe that serves as the vent for a common vent, combination waste and vent, horizontal and vertical wet vents or for branch vents, circuit vents and relief vents, (Section 906.2 of the Code) "the size shall not be less than ½ the required diameter of the drain served". Notice that the Code states that the vent must be ½ of the "required" diameter of the drain served. If an installer puts in a 4 inch drain where only a 3 inch drain was required, the vent would only need to be 1 ½" and not 2". If the vent that is being sized exceeds 40 feet in total developed length then the Code requires that it must be increased one pipe size for the entire length.

Stack Vents, Vent Stacks and Vent Headers (see definitions) have their own sizing Table, 906.1. These vents are sized on three different criteria: (1) Size of Soil or Waste Stack they serve (2) Total number of fixture units as determined from Table 709.1 and (3) Developed length measured from the vent connection to the open air. Vent Stacks are typically the parallel vent pipe provided for multi-story buildings over 5 branch intervals or more. A Stack Vent is the dry continuation of a vertical waste or soil pipe after it has picked up the last horizontal drainage branch and becomes a vent. Vent Headers are when we combine Stack Vents or Vent Stacks or both and take one vent to termination.

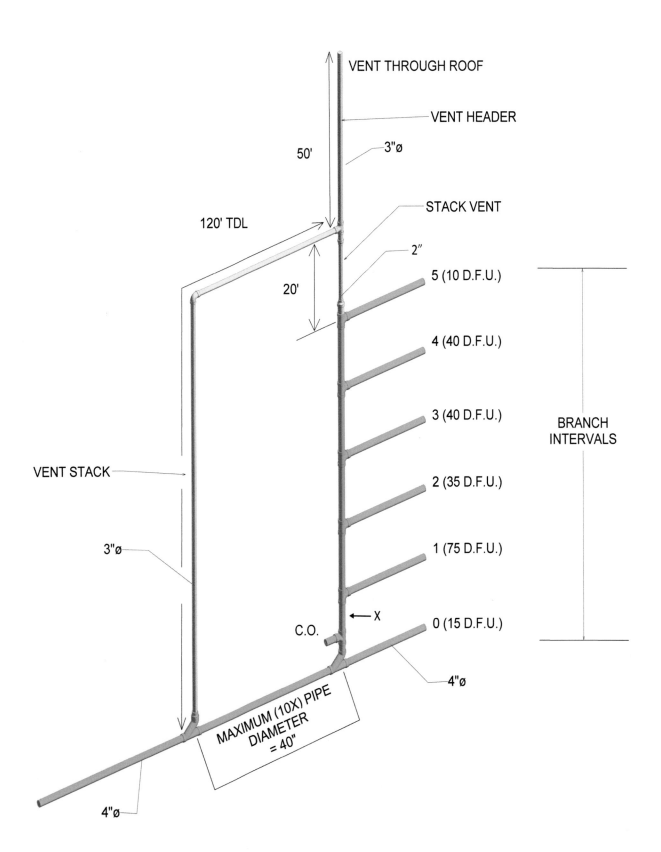

VENT THROUGH ROOF

VENT HEADER

3"ø

50'

120' TDL

STACK VENT

2"

20'

5 (10 D.F.U.)

4 (40 D.F.U.)

3 (40 D.F.U.)

BRANCH
INTERVALS

2 (35 D.F.U.)

1 (75 D.F.U.)

VENT STACK

3"ø

X

C.O.

0 (15 D.F.U.)

4"ø

MAXIMUM (10X) PIPE
DIAMETER
= 40"

4"ø

Diagram 101

De-coding chapter 9 of the IPC

In **Diagram 101**, the Vent Stack is required since the drainage stack is 5 branch intervals or more. The total drainage fixture units = 200 DFU. Note: The 15 dfu on the building drain is not considered in sizing the Stack (see footnote a. table 710.1(2)). To size Diagram 101: First size the drainage Stack using table 710.1(2). Total for stack greater than three branch Intervals: 200 dfu = 4 inch.

To size the Stack Vent (the dry vent extending from the drainage stack) use table 906.1. Start with the far left column of Table 906.1 and find where it shows the 4-inch diameter of the soil stack. There are 4 of them, choose the one that corresponds with the dfu in the adjacent right column to cover the total dfu of 200, which is the 320 dfu column. Stay on this horizontal line and continue looking to the right to find on the table the maximum developed length of vent. Since the Stack Vent length is 20 feet long, choose the 23-value column. The minimum size vent at the top of this column is 2".

To size the Vent Stack, we must know the developed length and dfu served. The developed length of the Vent Stack in this example is 120 feet. We already know the dfu is 200 from when we sized the drainage stack. Using the same column on Table 906.1 with the 4-inch soil stack, 200 dfu with a developed length of 120', the minimum vent size at the top of this column is 3 inch.

The Vent Stack is required to connect within 10 pipe diameters downstream of the drainage stack or 10 X 4 inch = 40 inches maximum. Vent Stacks can also connect to the vertical drainage stack between the lowest horizontal drainage branch and the building drain (see point **X**).

To size the Vent Header, use the same column we used to size the Vent Stack and add the additional length of 50 Feet. Now the total developed length is 170 feet. The table shows that the size would still be 3 inch.

TABLE 906.1
MAXIMUM DEVELOPED LENGTH OF STACK VENTS AND VENT STACKS

DIAMETER OF SOIL OR WASTE STACK (inches)	TOTAL FIXTURE UNITS BEING VENTED (dfu)	DIAMETER OF VENT							
		1 1/4	1 1/2	2	2 1/2	3	4	5	6
1 ¼	2	30 ft							
1 ½	8	50 ft	150	—	—	—	—	—	—
1 ½	10	30 ft	100						
2	12	-----	75	200					
2	20	30 ft	50	150	—	—	—	—	—
2 ½	42	26 ft	30	100	300				
3	10		42	150	360	1040			
3	21	—	32	110	270	810	—	—	—
3	53		27	94	230	680			
3	102		25	86	210	620			
4	43	—	---	35	85	250	980	—	—
4	140		---	27	65	200	750		
4	320			23	55	170	640		
4	540	—	—	21	50	150	580		—
5	190			---	28	82	320	990	
5	490				21	63	250	760	
5	940	—	—	—	18	53	210	670	—
5	1400				16	49	190	590	
6	500					33	130	400	1000
6	1100	—	—	—	—	26	100	310	780
6	2000					22	84	260	660

Branch vents are sized at ½ of the required drain served. Again, the required drain size must be known in order to correctly size these vents. Below you have an example in **Diagram 102** where there is a circuit vented bathroom group located on a horizontal branch sized in accordance with table 710.1(2). There are five vertical vents tied together with a common branch vent. The individual vents serving the two common vented lavatories are sized at one-half the required vertical drain size of 1 ½" (based on table 710.1(2) or 1 ¼" vent. Where the lower two individual double Lavatories tie together is a total of 4 dfu requiring a horizontal drain size of 2 inch allowing 1 ¼" branch vent. As you add the dfu of next two urinals, the total dfu is 8 requiring the drain to increase to 2 ½". This still allows a 1 ¼" vent (we do not count the WC in between the two urinals as it is vented by the circuit). The last vertical vent is the required dry vent for the circuit vent. We know that the size of the circuit vent is 3-inch minimum since the total dfu is 20. Section 906.2 of the Code allows this vent to be one-half the size of the required drain or 1 ½". The size of this vent remains 1 ½" and continues that size to where it would terminate outdoors, to an AAV, or to a stack or vent stack.

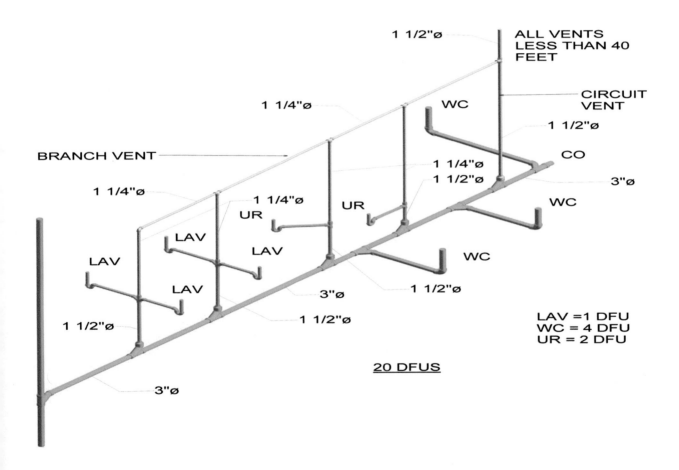

DIAGRAM 102
BRANCH VENTS

Minimum Vent size. In no case shall any vent be less than ½ of the diameter of the drain served or less than one and one quarter inch (1 1/4 inch).

Section and Table 909.1 of the Code. Trap to vent distances. "Each fixture trap shall have a protecting vent located so that the slope and the developed length in the fixture drain from the trap weir to the vent fitting are within the requirements set forth in Table 909.1"

This table is important to reference whether you have a single fixture that is individually or common vented or if you are using one of the wet venting systems discussed in this book or the Code. Most fixtures connected to a wet-vented system are still limited in the fixture drain length to the wet-vent connection as determined in Table 909.1. For example (See **photograph 8**) a shower fixture drain with a 2 inch trap sloped at a ¼ inch per foot connected to a circuit vent is limited to 8 feet from where it connects to the horizontal branch vent to the weir of the trap. If a fixture drain connecting to one of the wet venting systems is allowed by the rules of the vented system but exceeds the trap to vent distances, then it could still be permitted to connect as long as it is properly vented. Water closets are the exception to the trap to vent distance rule, the length of the fixture drain is unlimited for self-siphoning fixtures. Fixtures that are sized and permitted to be used on combination waste and vent systems are also unlimited since the waste and the vent are the same pipe.

Below is Table 909.1 of the International Plumbing Code.

TABLE 909.1

SIZE OF TRAP (inches)	SLOPE (inch per foot)	DISTANCE FROM TRAP (feet)
1 ¼	¼	5
1 ½	¼	6
2	¼	8
3	1/8	12
4	1/8	16

For SI: 1 inch =25.4mm, 1 foot =304.8mm, 1 inch per foot =83.3 mm/m.

Notice that the maximum slope in addition to the maximum distance for each size pipe is shown in the table. If a pipe exceeds the slope or distance shown in the table then the vent connection may fall below the weir of the trap causing a potential loss of trap seal. The developed length of the fixture drain is measured from the weir of trap to the vent fitting.

Section 909.2 of the Code. "The total fall in a fixture drain due to pipe slope shall not exceed the diameter of the fixture drain". Another way to remember trap to vent distances is by multiplying the length of the fixture drain by the slope of ¼". For example: 8 X ¼" = 2" which means 8 feet is the limit for 2 inch pipe.

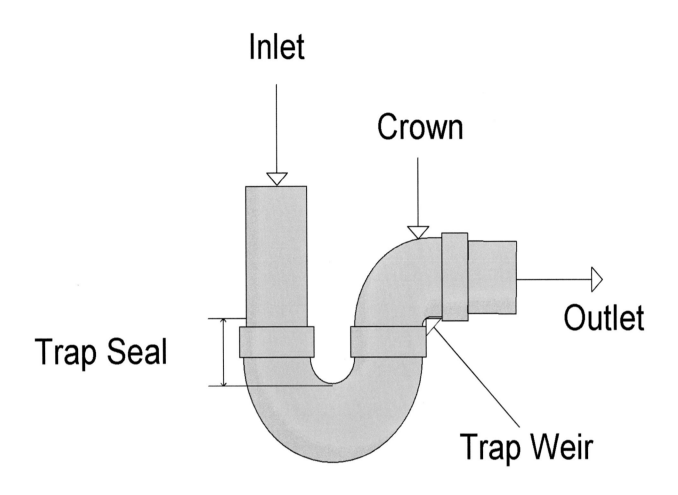

TRAP

DIAGRAM 103

In the above diagram (**Diagram 103**) notice the different parts of the trap. Venting systems are designed to help protect the trap from losing its seal. The inlet connects the fixture to the trap and the outlet becomes the fixture drain. The trap weir is the point where the water from the trap seal begins to travel from the outlet down the fixture drain. Some of the venting rules reference the different parts of the trap, so it is important to know exactly where these parts are.

De-coding chapter 9 of the IPC

Photograph 6 below illustrates the trap to vent distance on an individually vented fixture.

Trap to Vent Distance

Photograph 6

In the common vent below (**Photograph 7**), the trap to vent distance again is illustrated. It is measured from "weir of trap to the vent fitting"

Photograph 7

In the circuit vent below (**Photograph 8**), the shower fixture drain connected to the circuit vented branch (vent) is limited to the distances in table 909.1. In this example the fixture drain is 2 inch and would be limited to 8 feet.

Photograph 8

The trap to vent distance is always measured from the vent connection to the trap weir. In **Diagram 104**, the vent is connected through a combo fitting on its back. Notice the vent connection on the fitting is where the vent connects to the fixture drain.

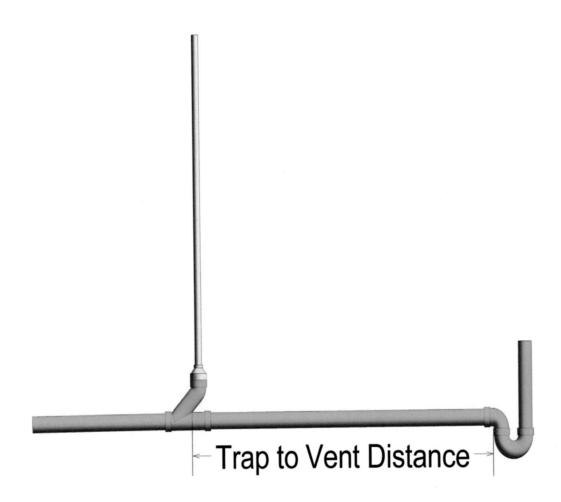

Trap to Vent Distance

DIAGRAM 104

Section 909.3 of the Code In addition to maximum distances from the vent to trap there are also "minimum" distances. If a distance is too short (Crown vent) the fixture trap may lose its seal through siphonage and can allow sewer gas to enter the building through the fixture. The trap seal (a minimum of 2 inches but not more than 4 inches of liquid seal) is what keeps the sewer gas from entering the building. In **Photographs 9**, **10** and **11** you can see an example of a crown vent in these field photos. In photograph **9** and **10**, the fixture is a 3-inch mop sink vented by an individual vent. Since the size of the pipe between the weir of the trap and the vent is 3 inch, the minimum distance is required to be 2 times (2X) the diameter of the pipe or in this case, 6 inches. In this example the installer glued the fittings hub to hub providing less than the required distance.

Photograph 9

The 3 inch pipe used in **Photograph 10** below to pipe the mop sink would require 6 inches of "developed length" between the trap weir and the vent connection in order to be accepted. Because the pipe is less than 6 inches, it would be considered a crown vent and is prohibited by 909.3 of the Code.

Photograph 10

Photograph 11 shows a commercial food grinder (on right) where the vent is taken off the top of the trap. This is another example of a violation of the code in a "crown vent". The vent would need to connect to the 2-inch fixture drain at least 4 inches (2 times the diameter of the drain) downstream of the trap to be accepted. The vent also offsets horizontally below the flood rim which is also prohibited by section 905.4 of the Code.

Photograph 11

3 Individual and Common vents

IPC Sections 910.1 and 911.1. These are the most common and simple venting methods you will see. Individual vents are as the name suggests, they typically vent an individual fixture. In some cases they vent two fixtures and then you have a common vent.

•**Individual Vent** "A pipe installed to vent a fixture trap and that connects with the vent system above the fixture served or terminates in the open air"

Photograph 12

Individual vents are sized to be one-half (1/2) the size of the required drain size of the fixture vented. The size of the drain is determined by Table 710.1(2) of the Code. **Photograph 12** illustrates a commercial lavatory in a public bathroom. The "carrier" is what the fixture will mount to on final installation. The upper cap on the Santee is the fixture drain. The lower cap is for a cleanout. A single lavatory could be piped on as small as 1 ¼" drain and 1 ¼" vent. Since 1 1/4" cast iron is not readily available, this installer used 2-inch pipe out of convenience.

Photograph 13

In **Photograph 13**, there are two individually vented sinks side by side. The sink on the left has a combo in the vertical position to vent the sink. Since the combo has a vent connection below the weir of the trap, this installation would not be accepted. The sink on the right used a Santee and is vented correctly.

●**Common Vent** "A vent connecting at the junction of two fixture drains or to a fixture *branch* and serving as a vent for both fixtures"

Diagram 105 The individual vent serving a common vent at the same level vent is sized at ½ of the required vertical drain. Each LAV is one dfu according to table 709.1, so the vertical drain is required to be 1 ½" by table 710.1(2). The vent would have to be ½ of the required drain but not less than 1 ¼".

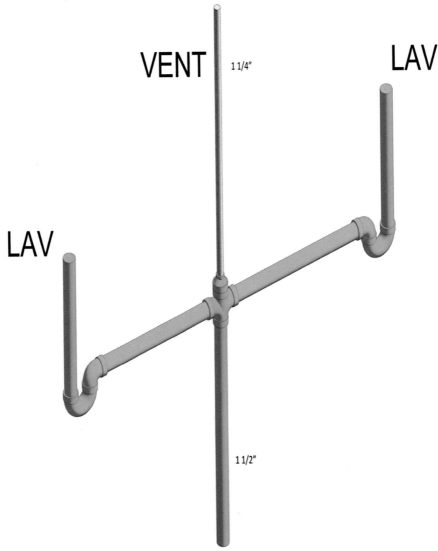

COMMON VENT AT SAME LEVEL

DIAGRAM 105

An individual vent can also serve as a Common Vent for two trapped fixtures. Common Vents are vertical with both fixtures connecting at the same level, two fixtures connecting different levels or on a horizontal fixture branch using a double pattern fitting. **Photograph 14** shows back to back fixtures common vented at the same level. Here the installer used double pattern fittings on the water closets. **Section 909.2 of the Code** permits connections below the weir of the trap on water closets. A double Santee was correctly used for the back to back floor drains.

Photograph 14

Photograph 15 below is a commercial common vent on the same level serving side-by-side drinking fountains.

Photograph 15

Photograph 16 below shows a correctly installed common vent on the same level. The fitting used here is a double fixture fitting but it could have also been a double Santee to connect the two fixtures. Either fitting is appropriate.

Photograph 16

Common Vents at different levels. Sizing the "common" piping between the upper fixture and the lower fixture. That section of pipe is sized according to Table 911.3. The individual vent serving the common vent is sized at ½ of the required drain but not less than 1 ¼ ". The Code also states that the upper fixture may not be a water closet. **Diagram 106** the sizing at point A is determined from Table 710.1(2) based on dfu total for one branch interval. The sizing at point B is based on Table 911.3. The individual vent serving the common vent at point C is sized at ½ the largest required drain but not less than 1 ¼".

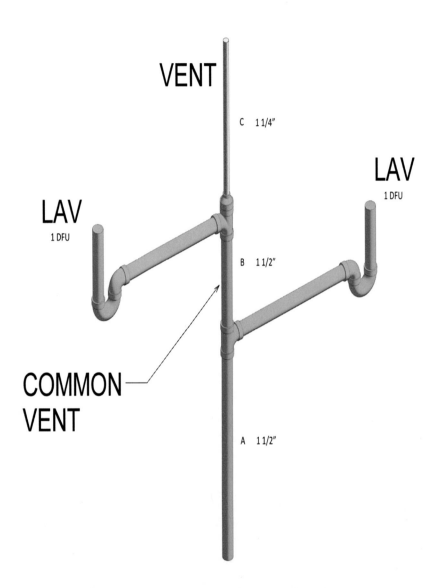

COMMON VENT AT DIFFERENT LEVELS

DIAGRAM 106

Photograph 17. Common Vent connecting at different levels. The piping between the upper fixture drain and the lower fixture drain is sized to Table 911.3

COMMON VENT AT
DIFFERENT LEVELS

Photograph 17

Photograph 18 Common Vent connecting at different levels. The piping between the upper fixture drain and the lower fixture drain is sized to Table 911.3. Here the installer continued the larger size of 3-inch vent for a clean out.

Photograph 18

Common Vent Sizing. Table 911.3 of the Code shall only be used for sizing the common vent between the upper and lower fixtures for connection at different levels.

TABLE 911.3
COMMON VENT SIZES

PIPE SIZE (inches)	MAXIMUM DISCHARGE FROM UPPER FIXTURE DRAIN (dfu)
1 1/2	1
2	4
2 ½ - 3	6

Sizing of other Common Vent Systems: Tables 709.1, 709.2 and 710.1(2) are located in chapter 7 of the 2015 International Plumbing Code and are necessary for sizing the drain pipes so we can size the vent systems. The size of the drain must be known in order to size your vents accordingly. The tables are also available on page 49 and page 50 of this manual for your convenience and reference.

For the pipe sizing of the fixtures connected using the other common vented methods other than common vented fixtures with connections at different levels, first size the drain pipe to table 710.1(2) of the Code. Then size the vent serving the common vented pipe at a minimum of ½ of that pipe size but not less than 1 ¼".

For example the two bathtubs in **Diagram 107** are valued at 2 dfu each according to table 709.1 or 4 total dfu. Table 710.1(2) says that 2-inch pipe can carry up to 6 dfu so 2 inch would be the correct pipe size. The vent serving the 2 inch fixture branch is sized at ½ the required drain but not less than 1 ¼". In this case the minimum vent required would be 1 ¼".

Diagram 107. A common vent on the horizontal fixture branch. A double pattern fitting is required to connect the two fixtures. The fixture branch is sized by Table 710.1(2) and the individual vent serving the fixture branch is sized at 1/2 of the fixture branch but not less than 1 ¼". Because a common vent can only serve two fixtures, the individual vent serving it must be dry and may not receive the discharge of any other fixtures.

COMMON VENT

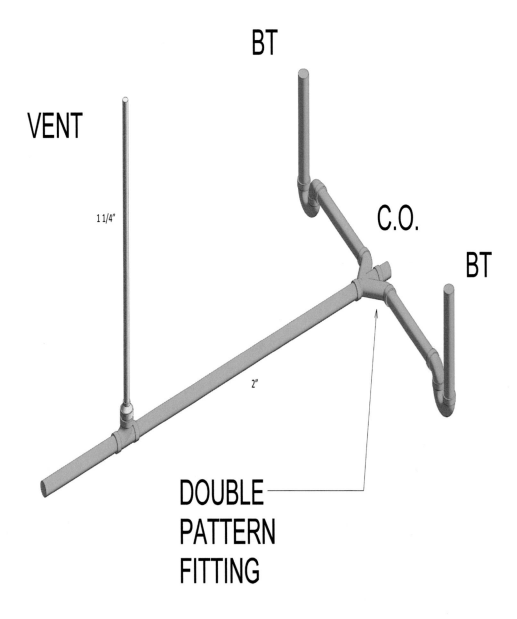

DIAGRAM 107

Photograph 19 A correctly installed common vented back-to-back water closets installation.

Photograph 19

Photograph 20 A correctly installed common vented back-to-back water closets installation.

Photograph 20

Photograph 21 A common vented back-to-back water closet carrier.

Photograph 21

Photograph 22 A correctly vented Common vented back-to-back sinks using a double pattern fitting.

Photograph 22

TABLE 709.1 DRAINAGE FIXTURE UNITS FOR FIXTURES AND GROUPS

FIXTURE TYPE	DRAINAGE FIXTURE UNIT	MIN SIZE OF TRAP (inches)
Automatic clothes washers, commercial[a,g]	3	2
Automatic clothes washers, residential[g]	2	2
Bathroom group as defined in Section 202 (1.6 gpf water closet)[f]	5	—
Bathroom group as defined in Section 202 (water closet flushing greater than 1.6 gpf)[f]	6	—
Bathtub[b] (with or without overhead shower or whirlpool attachments)	2	$1^1/_2$
Bidet	1	$1^1/_4$
Combination sink and tray	2	1 1/2
Dental lavatory	1	$1^1/_4$
Dental unit or cuspidor	1	$1^1/_4$
Dishwashing machine[c],domestic	2	$1^1/_2$
Drinking fountain	1/2	$1^1/_4$
Emergency floor drain	0	2
Floor drains[h]	2h	2
Floor sinks	Note h	2
Kitchen sink, domestic	2	$1^1/_2$
Kitchen sink, domestic with food waste disposer and/or dishwasher	2	$1^1/_2$
Laundry tray (1 or 2 compartments)	2	$1^1/_2$
Lavatory	1	$1^1/_4$
Shower (based on the total flow rates) Flow rate: 5.7 gpm or less / Greater than 5.7 to 12.3 gpm / Greater than 12.3 to 25.8 gpm / Greater than 25.8 to 55.6 gpm	2 / 3 / 5 / 6	1 ½ / 2 / 3 / 4
Service sink	2	$1^1/_2$
Sink	2	$1^1/_2$
Urinal	4	Note d
Urinal, 1 gallon per flush or less	2e	Note d
Urinal, non-water supplied	1/2	Note d
Wash sink (circular or multiple) each set of faucets	2	$1^1/_2$
Water Closet, flushometer tank, public or private	4e	Note d
Water Closet, private (1.6 gpf)	3e	Note d
Water Closet private (greater than 1.6 gpf)	4e	Note d
Water closet, public (1.6 gpf)	4e	Note d
Water closet, public (flushing greater than 1.6 gpf)	6e	Note d

FOOTNOTES FOR TABLE 709.1

For SI: 1 inch = 25.4 mm, 1 gallon = 3.785 L, gpf = gallon per flushing cycle, gpm = gallon per minute.

a. For traps larger than 3 inches, use Table 709.2.
b. A showerhead over a bathtub or whirlpool bathtub attachment does not increase the drainage fixture unit value.
c. See Sections 709.2 through 709.4.1 for methods of computing unit value of fixtures not listed in this table or for rating of devices with intermittent flows.
d. Trap size shall be consistent with the fixture outlet size.
e. For the purpose of computing loads on building drains and sewers, water closets and urinals shall not be rated at a lower drainage fixture unit unless the lower values are confirmed by testing.
f. For fixtures added to a bathroom group, add the dfu value of those additional fixtures to the bathroom group fixture count.
g. See Section 406.3 for sizing requirements for fixture drain, branch drain, and drainage stack for an automatic clothes washer standpipe.
h. See Sections 709.4 and 709.4.1.

TABLE 709.2
DRAINAGE FIXTURE UNITS FOR FIXTURE DRAINS OR TRAPS

FIXTURE DRAIN OR TRAP SIZE (inches)	DRAINAGE FIXTURE UNIT VALUE
$1\frac{1}{4}$	1
$1\frac{1}{2}$	2
2	3
$2\frac{1}{2}$	4
3	5
4	6

TABLE 710.1(2)
HORIZONTAL FIXTURE BRANCHES AND STACKS[a]

Diameter of Pipe (inches)	Total for horizontal branch	Total for one branch interval	Total for stack 3 branch intervals or less	Total for stack greater than 3 branch intervals
$1\frac{1}{2}$	3	2	4	8
2	6	6	10	24
2 1/2	12	9	20	42
3	20	20	48	72
4	160	90	240	500
5	360	200	540	1100
6	620	350	960	1900

a. Does not include branches of the building drain. Refer to table 710.1(1) of the Code

Diagram 108. A common vent fixture branch may also connect to a vertical stack as shown in. A common mistake with this type of venting is using a wye fitting (see **photograph 23**) instead of a double pattern fitting.

COMMON VENT

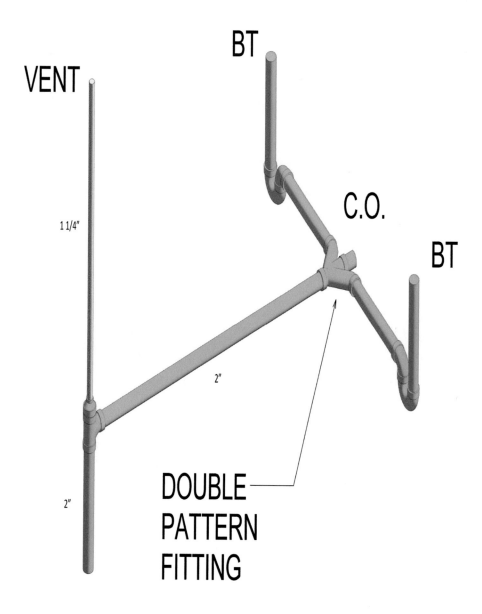

DIAGRAM 108

Photograph 23 An **incorrectly** common vented installation. A double pattern is required to connect the two fixtures.

Photograph 23

Photograph 24 The fixtures from **Photograph 23** are now vented correctly with a double pattern fitting.

Photograph 24

In **Photograph 25** the side by side fixtures valued at 2 dfu are connected to an 1 ½" vented fixture branch which would require a **double pattern fitting** to be vented correctly as a common vent.

Photograph 25

4 WET VENTING

With most of the venting methods we are covering in this book, the theory of wet venting can be put in simple terms. When considering horizontal wet venting, the bottom half of the pipe is the waste and the top half of the pipe is air (or the vent). With vertical wet-venting piping, the waste tends to circle the inside of the piping and the center of the pipe is air. The piping with both methods is sized so that a single pipe can act as both the waste and the vent.

IPC Section 912. Many times when I ask an installer or designer when inspecting a plumbing installation is what type of venting system they are using, they will reply, "wet venting". Although the installation I'm looking at the time may not be a true "wet vent" as defined in section 912 of the IPC, their response may be correct (in theory) since many of the venting systems in chapter 9 of the Code (common venting, waste stack venting, circuit venting, combination waste and vent and single stack venting) are all in essence a type of wet-venting. But when designing a plumbing system to this section of the IPC, "wet venting" is a term specific to <u>bathroom groups.</u> A "bathroom group" is defined in the Code as: "A group of fixtures consisting of a water closet, lavatory, bathtub or shower, including or excluding a bidet, an *emergency floor drain* or both. Such fixtures are located together on the same floor level." This definition is critical to installing a wet vent system correctly. If an installer tries to use a fixture such as a drinking fountain or a hand sink to "wet vent" a water closet, this would not be acceptable since the drinking fountain or the hand sink is not a fixture defined in the Code as part of a bathroom group. Only fixtures defined as a bathroom group may be used in the wet venting methods in this section.

Wet Venting is separated into either "horizontal" or "vertical" and is limited to <u>any combination of fixtures</u> within **two bathroom groups**. So if you look at the definition of the "bathroom group" of the Code, you may use *any combination* of two groups together on one wet venting system and be Code compliant.

- **Bathroom Group** "A group of fixtures consisting of a water closet, lavatory, bathtub or shower, including or excluding a bidet, an *emergency floor drain* or both. Such fixtures are located together on the same floor level".

It is not necessary to have *all* the components of two bathroom groups in the wet vent system, you could have less than the total amount of fixtures in two bathroom groups. But you may not exceed the total number of water closets; bathtubs or showers, lavatories, bidets or floor drains in two bathroom groups. For example, a bathroom group could be one water closet, one bathtub, one shower, one bidet and two lavatories (a typical master bathroom in a luxury home). Or you could have two water closets, two lavatories and two bathtubs (back to back standard bathrooms). Another example would be to have two toilets and two lavatories and two floor drains (typical commercial side by side bathroom). These examples could all be wet vented using section 912 of the Code. If you were to have only one water closet on a wet vented system but wanted to have two showers and a bathtub, this would not meet Code. The simple elimination of a water closet from the formula does not allow an addition of another fixture above the definition of the two bathroom groups.

It is important to note that horizontal and vertical wet venting is not the same as a vertical or horizontal "pipe" as defined in chapter 2 of the Code. These wet vent systems follow strict criteria separate from the other definitions in the Code. It this case, a horizontal wet vent would not be a legal horizontal wet vent if it has a vertical offset less than 45 degrees from the horizontal (definition of a horizontal pipe). The same with the vertical wet vent, it may not be a legal vertical wet vent if it offsets more than 45 degrees from the horizontal.

•Horizontal Wet Vent "A horizontal vent system using any combination of fixtures within two bathroom groups located on the same floor level. The horizontal wet vent begins at the connection of the required dry vent connection and extends downstream to the last horizontally connected wet vented fixture drain. Each wet vented fixture drain connected shall connect independently and horizontally to the horizontal wet vent. The horizontal wet vent may not have vertical offsets. The required dry vent shall be an individual or common vent for any bathroom group fixture except for an emergency floor drain. Not more than one fixture may connect upstream from the dry vent connection to the horizontal wet vent"

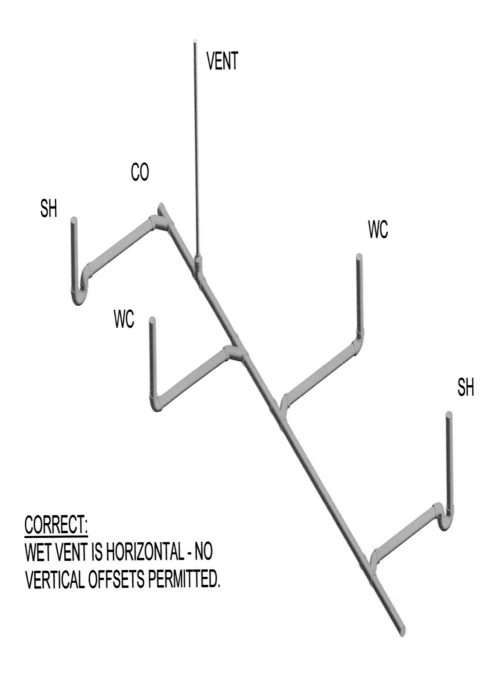

CORRECT:
WET VENT IS HORIZONTAL - NO
VERTICAL OFFSETS PERMITTED.

DIAGRAM 109

With horizontal wet venting, the fixtures connected must enter the wet vent on the same horizontal elevation as the horizontal pipe acting as the wet vent and the horizontal pipe acting as the wet vent may not have vertical offsets. Vertical offsets could interfere with the intended design and function of the system. Notice that dry vent connections may be made with a Santee on its back. If the vent connection to the system has a fixture connected then it shall be made with a long pattern drainage (wye and 1/8 or combo) fitting on its back.

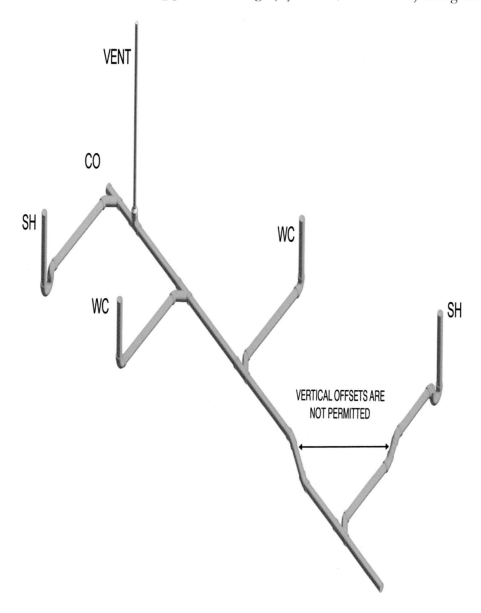

DIAGRAM 110
INCORRECT WET VENT

Examples of correct Horizontal Wet-Venting

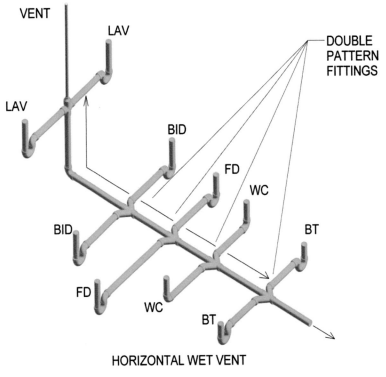

HORIZONTAL WET VENT

DIAGRAM 111

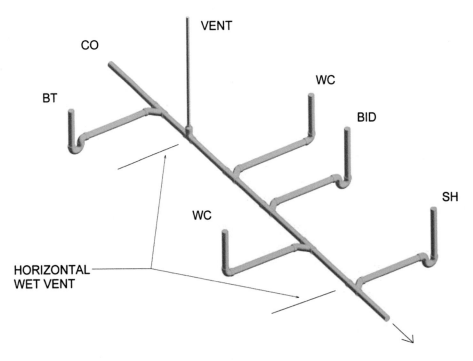

DIAGRAM 112

Table 912.3
Wet Vent Sizing

WET VENT PIPE SIZE (inches)	DRAINAGE FIXTURE UNIT (dfu)
1 1/2	1
2	4
2 1/2	6
3	12

Wet Vent Sizing To size wet venting systems in this section, first determine the size of the wet-vented section of piping using Table 709.1 and Table 912.3. The dry vent serving the wet vent is required to be ½ of the largest required drain size but not less than 1 ¼". In **Diagram 113** below, the largest required diameter of the wet vent is 3 inch which would then require a 1 ½" dry vent.

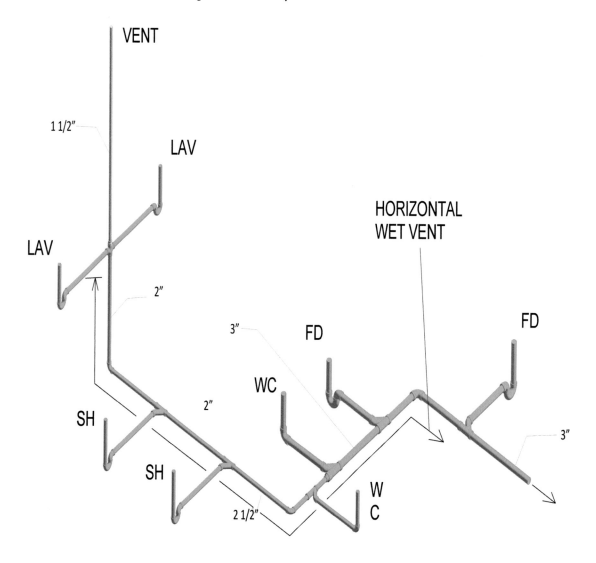

DIAGRAM 113

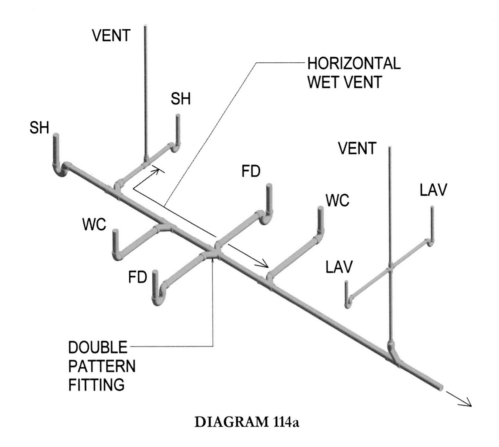

VENT

SH

SH

HORIZONTAL
WET VENT

VENT

FD

LAV

WC

WC

LAV

FD

DIAGRAM 114a

DOUBLE
PATTERN
FITTING

VENT

1 1/2"ø

2"ø

SH

HORIZONTAL
WET VENT

1 1/4"ø

SH

VENT

LAV

FD

WC

WC

LAV

3"ø

LAV

FD

1 1/2"ø

3"ø

DIAGRAM 114b

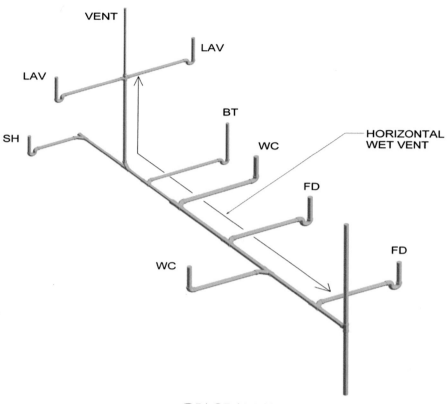

DIAGRAM 115a

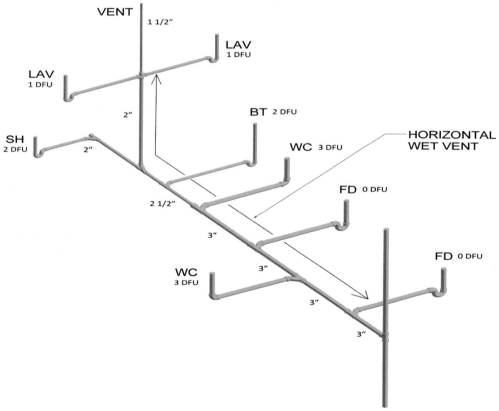

DIAGRAM 115b

Although section 912.2.1 of the Code states that only <u>one</u> fixture may discharge upstream of the required dry vent, the same section also states that the required dry vent may be for a common vent as shown in the example in **Diagram 116** below. The back-to-back bathtubs are a legal way to vent the horizontal wet vent in this installation when using a double pattern fitting upstream of the dry vent.

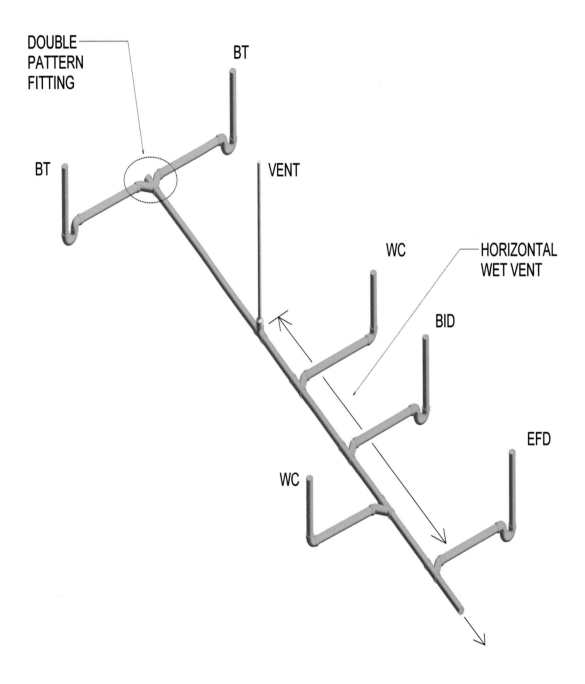

DIAGRAM 116

DIAGRAM 117 below shows an **incorrect** example of common venting to vent the horizontal wet vent. Since there is already a common vent (connection at different levels) venting the horizontal wet vent, there cannot be any other fixtures upstream of the vent.

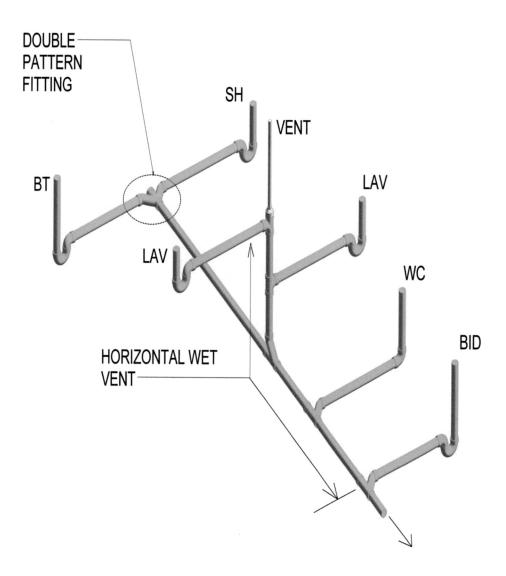

DIAGRAM 117
INCORRECT WET VENT

DIAGRAM 118 below shows a **correct** common vent used to vent the horizontal wet vent.

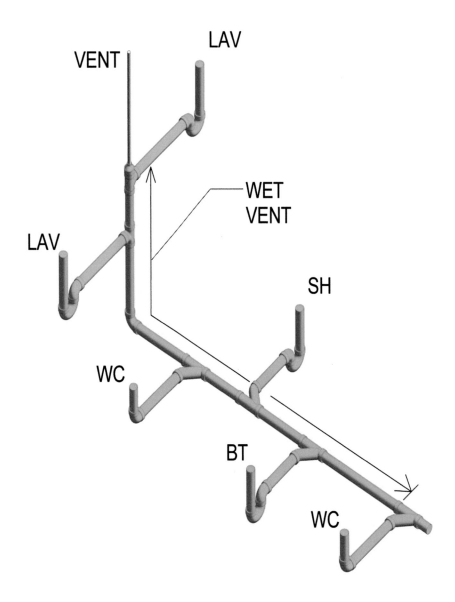

DIAGRAM 118
CORRECTLY VENTED WITH A COMMON VENT

DIAGRAM 119 is an **incorrect** horizontal wet vent with too many fixtures of the same kind. Section 912.1 of the Code permits "any combination of fixtures within <u>two bathroom groups</u>"

●**Bathroom Group** "A group of fixtures consisting of a water closet, lavatory, bathtub or shower, including or excluding a bidet, an *emergency floor drain* or both. Such fixtures are located together on the same floor level".

Two bathroom groups include two water closets, two lavatories, two bathtubs or two showers (one of each but not both) two bidets and two emergency floor drains. Below the diagram shows three lavatories, two bathtubs and a shower.. which would not be permitted by Code. You may only have a bathtub and a shower, two bathtubs or two showers and two lavatories for this to be an acceptable installation.

TOO MANY FIXTURES OF SAME TYPE

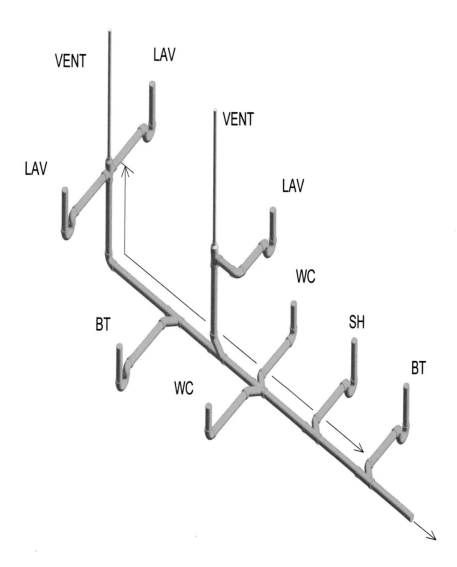

DIAGRAM 119

In **Diagram 120** we have a correctly installed horizontal wet vent. The emergency floor drain at first may appear to be upstream and a violation of 912.2.1. The floor drain is actually wet vented by the common vented lavatories and this example would be an acceptable installation.

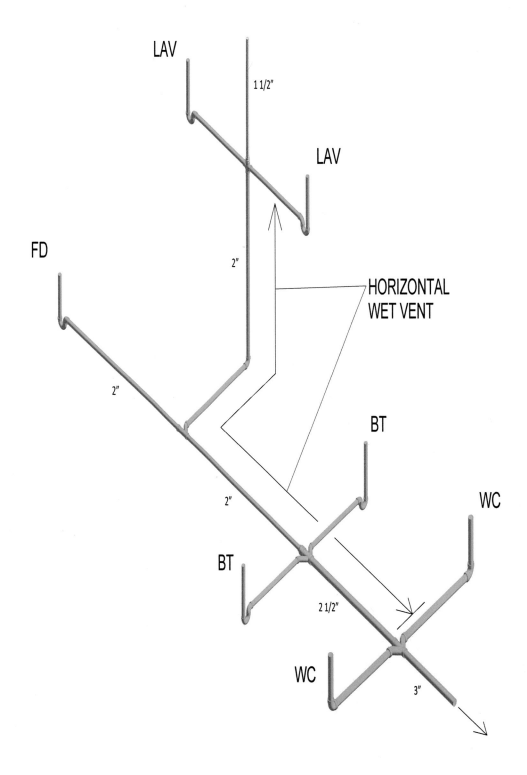

DIAGRAM 120

Photograph 26 This **incorrect** horizontal wet vent has a water closet entering on the vertical. Section 912.1 of the Code requires all fixtures to enter the wet vent on the horizontal.

Photograph 26

Photograph 27 This **incorrect** horizontal wet vent has a <u>dry vent</u> serving an emergency floor drain and a violation of Section 912.2.1 of the Code.

Photograph 27

Photograph 28 This installation is similar to the previous in **Photograph 27** where the emergency floor drain is the upper fixture. Here the EFD is wet-vented by the lavatory and would be accepted as a horizontal wet vent by Code.

Photograph 28

Photograph 29 This **incorrect** horizontal wet vent had a "double fixture fitting" on its side to pick up the back to back floor drains. Double fixture fittings are not the same as a "double pattern" fitting.

Photograph 29

Notice the difference in the double fixture fitting compared to the double pattern fitting

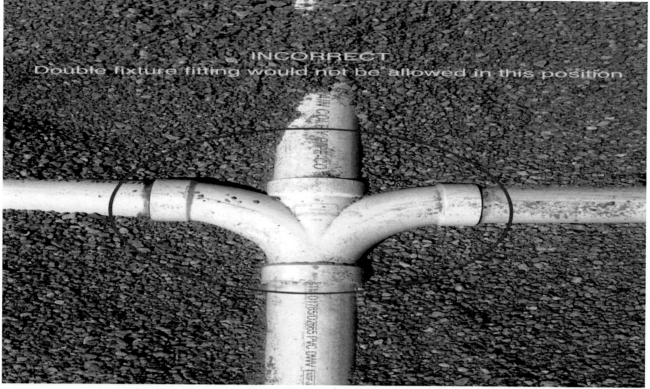

Photograph 30a

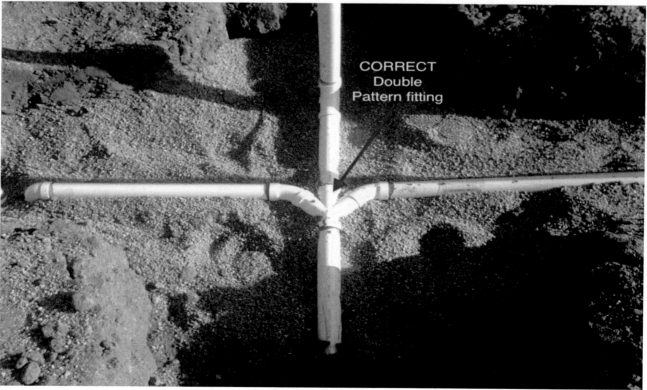

Photograph 30b

Photograph 31 A commercial installation of a horizontal wet vent where the lavatory is wet venting the water closet.

Photograph 31

Diagram 121 is an example of a simple horizontal wet vent where the BT (bathtub) trap weir exceeded the trap to vent distance from Table 909.1. This fixture is still permitted to discharge into the wet vent but must be provided with an additional vent.

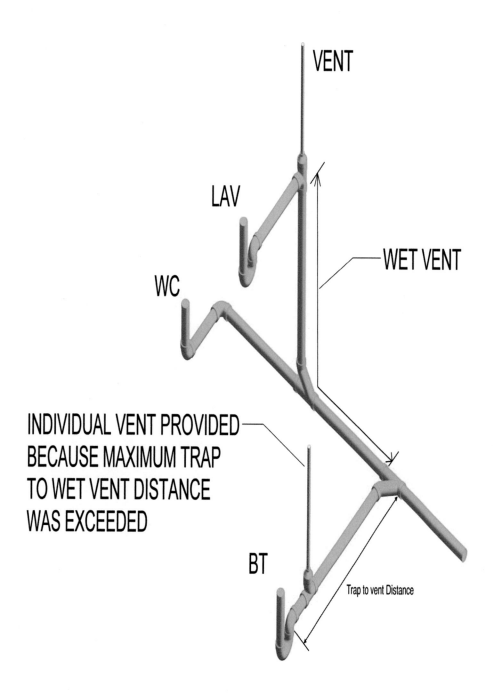

DIAGRAM 121

Photographs 32 and 33 A single bathroom that is wet vented. Not all of the components of the definition of "bathroom group" have to be included in order to have a wet vent. "Any combination of fixtures within two bathroom groups located on the same floor"

Photograph 32

Photograph 33

•**Vertical Wet Vent Definition:** "A vertical vent system using any combination of fixtures within two bathroom groups located on the same floor level. The vertical wet vent begins at the connection of the required dry vent connection and extends downstream to the lowest fixture drain connection. Each wet vented fixture drain shall connect independently to the vertical wet vent. Water closets shall connect at the same elevation and shall be the lowest fixtures on the vertical wet vent. Other fixtures drains shall connect above or at the same elevation as the water closets. The required dry vent shall be an individual or common vent.

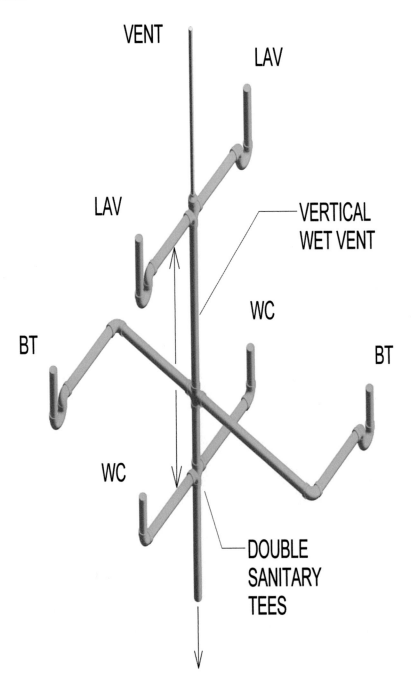

DIAGRAM 122

Vertical wet venting limits the same amount and type of fixtures as the horizontal wet venting. The main differences to remember here is that your water closet must be the lower most fixture and with *two* water closets, they must enter the vertical wet vent at the same level. This is usually achieved using a double fixture fitting, double sanitary tee (see section 706.3 "exception" for limitations on double sanitary tees) or double wye and 1/8 bend or combo fitting. Other fixtures may enter the vertical wet vent at the same elevation as the water closets but not below them. This is achieved usually through a side inlet fitting that is designed to allow a water closet and another fixture to connect and drain through the same fitting.

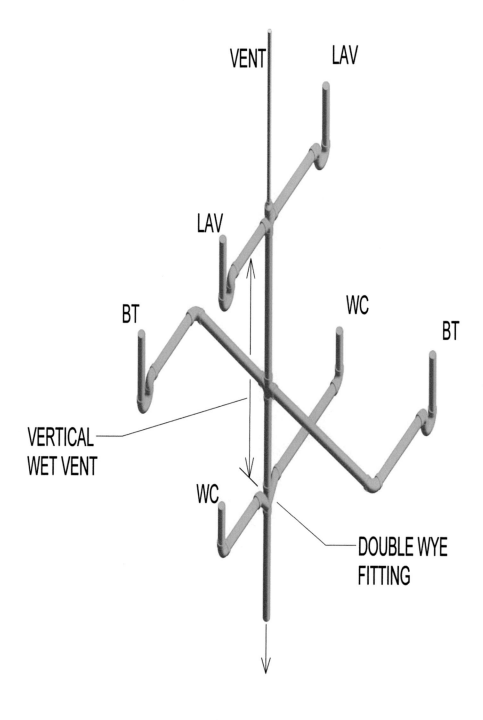

DIAGRAM 123

The water closet must be located as the lower most fixture. Other fixtures may connect at the same level but not below.

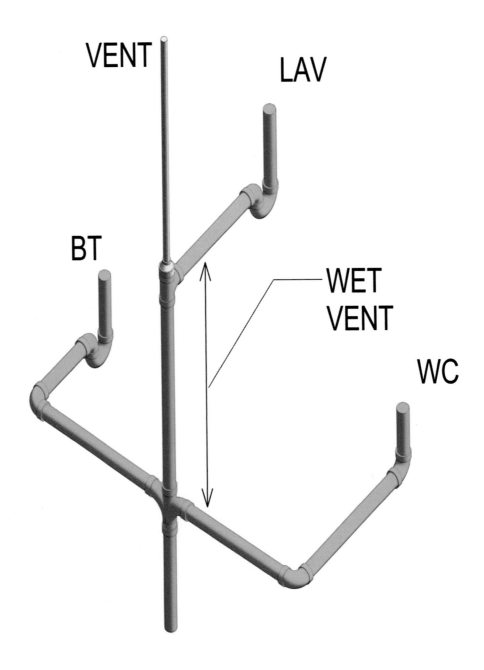

DIAGRAM 124

Vertical Wet Vent Sizing To size wet venting systems in this section, first determine the <u>largest</u> required size of the wet-vented section of piping using Table 709.1 and Table 912.3. The dry vent serving the wet vent is required to be ½ of the required drain size but not less than 1 ¼". In **Diagram 125** below, the largest required diameter of the drain is 3 inch which would then require a 1 ½" dry vent.

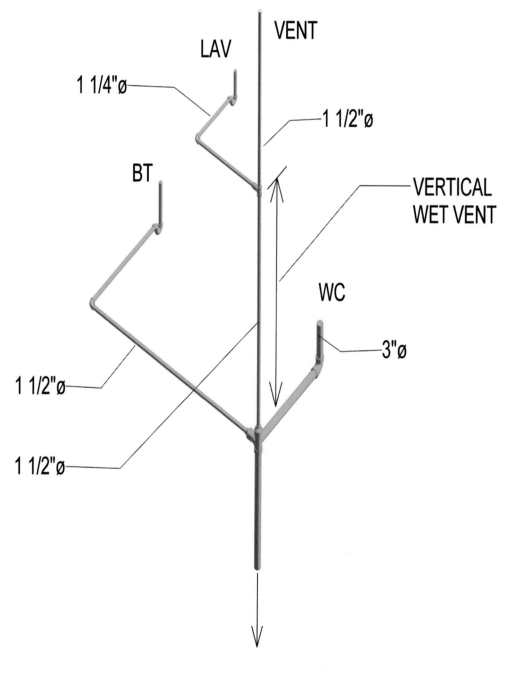

DIAGRAM 125

Diagram 126 When sizing the wet vent the minimum size of the required drain must be known. Because any drain line serving a water closet must be a minimum of 3 inch, this size must be used even if 2 inch can handle the total drainage fixture load (dfu). Since 3 inch is the minimum drain required, 1 ½" is the minimum required dry vent. The piping in between (wet vent) is sized on the total dfu and Table 912.3.

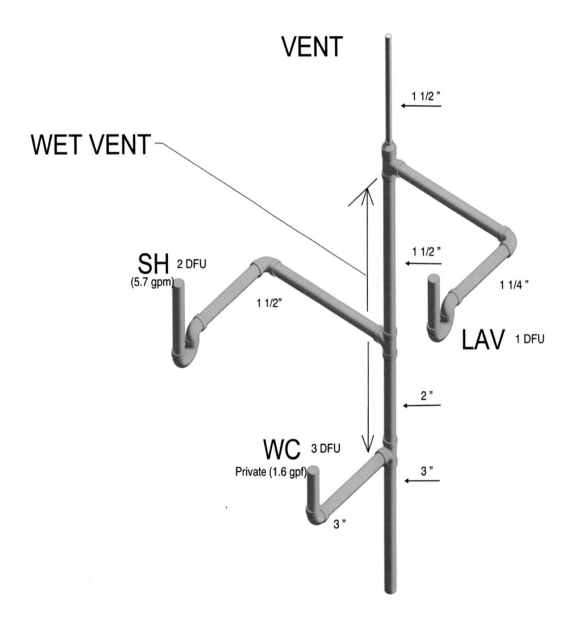

DIAGRAM 126

5 COMBINATION WASTE AND VENT

Section 915 of the Code. Combination Waste and Vent is one of the most versatile methods allowed by code. Properly designed and installed, this system is very helpful in large areas where there are few options to run a vent. These systems are typically used for floor drains or floor sinks and often for island sinks. Although a popular method, it is also one that can have leave an installer frustrated if not designed properly. As with any of the venting systems in the Code, the rules of the system must be followed in order to properly install the system. This system is used for fixtures producing only "waste". No "solids" are permitted to discharge into the system and the system shall not receive the discharge of a food waste disposer or clinical sink.

•**Combination Waste and Vent** "A specially designed system of waste piping embodying the horizontal wet venting of one or more sinks, lavatories, drinking fountains or floor drains by means of a common waste and vent pipe adequately sized to provide free movement of air above the flow line of the drain"

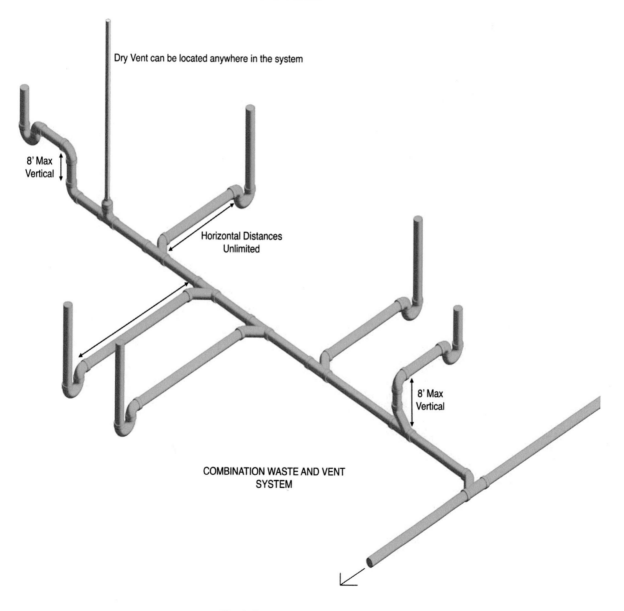

DIAGRAM 127

A combination waste and vent system may be a system with a few or many fixtures, or it may only be <u>one</u> fixture. The system shall have a vent, located anywhere in the system or the system or fixture must connect to a horizontal drain that is properly vented on the same floor with one of the methods specified in Chapter 9 of the Code. The only vertical portion of the combo w/v system may be a "fixture drain" between a fixture and the horizontal combination waste and vent system. The vertical pipe is limited to 8 feet. Horizontal piping on a combination waste and vent sized to Table 915.2.2 is not limited in length as the drain and the vent are the same pipe. A combination waste and vent pipe is limited to ½ inch per foot slope.

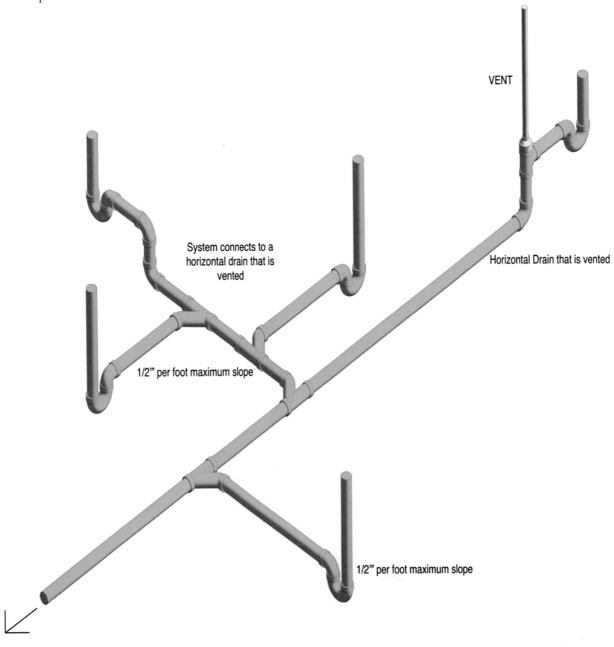

DIAGRAM 128

Photograph 34 A combination waste and vent system for a mechanical room. The required vent is located at the end of the system and can also act as the full size clean out for the line.

Photograph 34

Photograph 35 The two floor drains below connect to a horizontal drain that is vented. Each floor drain is considered its own combination waste and vent system and is sized to Table 915.2.2. A 2-inch pipe is the smallest pipe allowed on a combination waste and vent system.

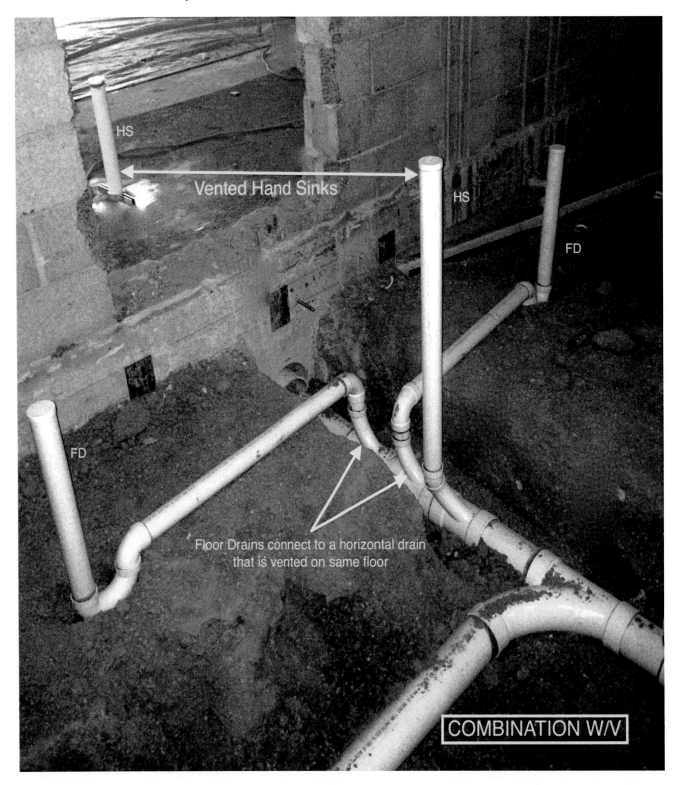

Photograph 35

Photograph 36 The emergency floor drain below is a single fixture vented by a combination waste and vent connected to a horizontal drain that is properly vented. The trap to vent distance is unlimited when the pipe is sized to Table 915.2.2.

Photograph 36

Photograph 37 A cast iron hub and spigot combination waste and vent system.

Photograph 37

Photograph 38 The horizontal distance is unlimited when sized to table 915.2.2

Photograph 38

Photograph 39 Although this might look like an incorrect common vent, it is actually an individually vented shower. The emergency floor drain is connected as a combination waste and vent to a horizontal drain that is vented. This installation would be accepted by code.

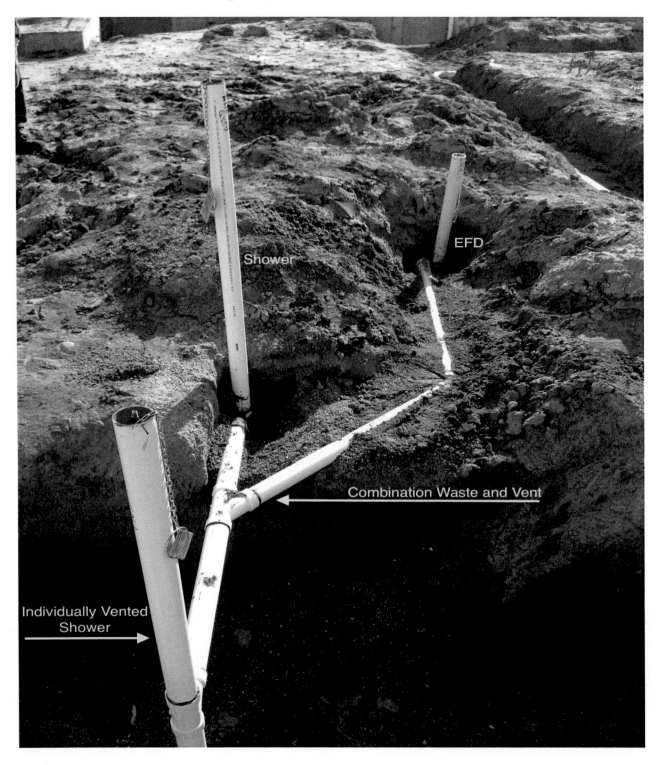

Photograph 39

TABLE 915.2.2
SIZE OF COMBINATION WASTE AND VENT PIPE

DIAMETER PIPE (inches)	MAXIMUM NUMBER OF DRAINAGE FIXTURE UNITS (dfu)	
	Connecting to a horizontal branch or stack	Connecting to a building drain or building subdrain
2	3	4
2 1/2	6	26
3	12	31
4	20	50
5	160	250
6	360	575

Table 915.2.2 Use Table 709.1 to determine fixture units load value of the individual fixtures then size the combination waste and vent pipe to Table 915.2.2. The dry vent serving the combination waste and vent will be sized at ½ of the total drainage fixture load of the system.

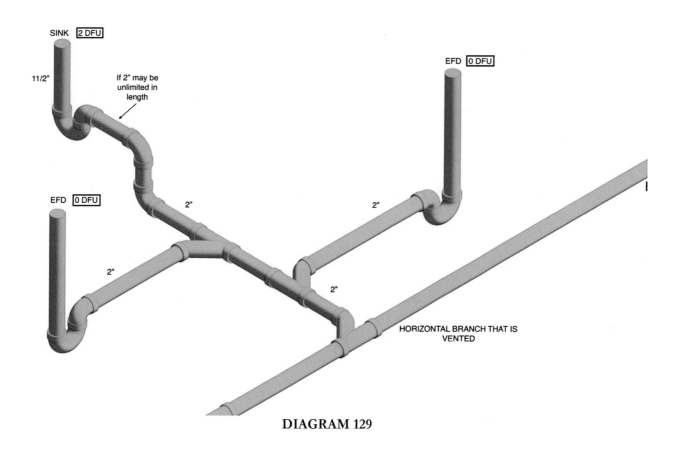

DIAGRAM 129

Diagram 129 The 2-inch vertical combination waste and vent pipes serving the sink remains 2 inch through the 2-inch elbow until it becomes horizontal again all the way to the fixture trap allowing unlimited length. **Diagram 130** shows a sized combination waste and vent system connected to a horizontal branch. Notice that 2-inch is the smallest size available for combination waste and vent in Table 915.2.2. The dry vent serving the system is based at ½ of the largest required drain size based on Table 915.2.2.

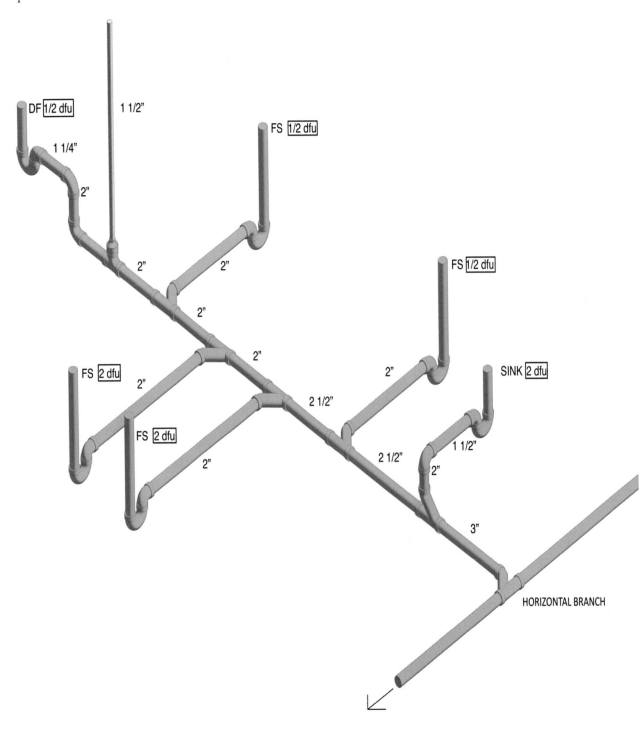

DIAGRAM 130

Diagram 131 The horizontal piping connecting the trap may become a "fixture drain" (Section 915.2.5 of the Code) and may be sized for the trap size outlet from Table 709.1. The trap to vent distance would be measured along the horizontal developed length from the "vent" (combination waste and vent) to the weir of the trap and be limited in length to Table 909.1.

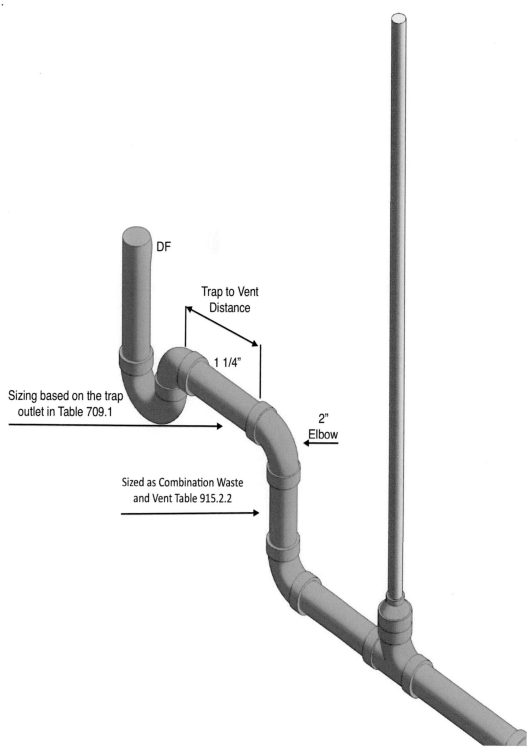

DIAGRAM 131

The fixture drain could also remain the same size required by Table 915.2.2 all the way to the trap and be unlimited in length. When sized to Table 915.2.2 it would be considered a continuation of the combination waste and vent pipe.

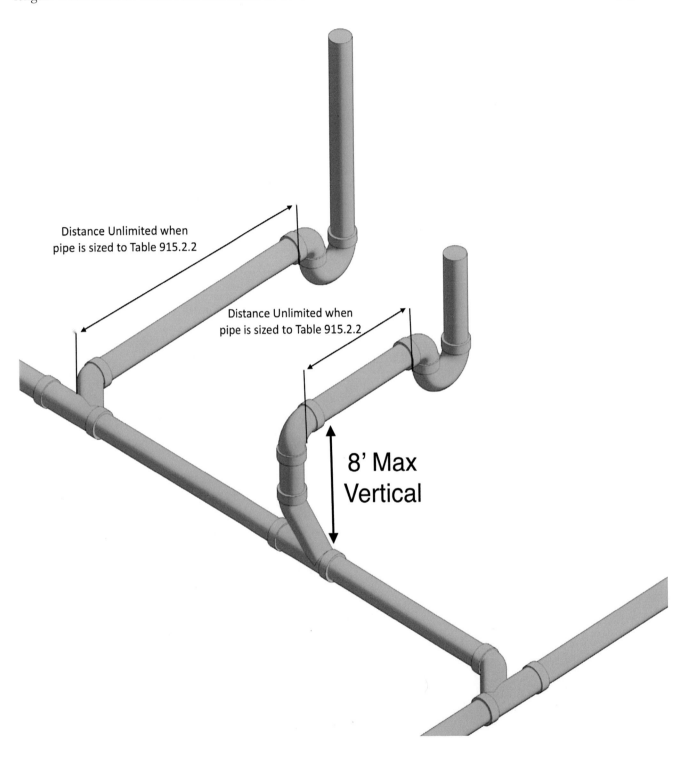

DIAGRAM 132

6 CIRCUIT VENTING

Section 914 of the Code Circuit venting is an effective way to vent large bathroom groups or large groups of fixtures. A maximum of eight fixtures may be vented by a single <u>dry vent</u>. This dry vent may not receive the discharge from any other fixtures and shall be located between the two upper most connected circuit vented fixtures. Each circuit vented fixture drain shall connect horizontally to the circuit vented branch.

●**Circuit Vent** "A vent that connects to a horizontal drainage *branch* and vents two traps to a maximum of eight traps or trapped fixtures connected into a battery"

If there are more than eight fixtures circuit vented fixtures on a branch then another circuit vent can connect to accommodate the extra fixtures **(Multiple circuit vented branches). Additional fixtures** other than the circuit vented fixtures may connect to the circuit vented branch as long as they are either individually or common vented.

A **relief vent** shall be provided for any circuit vented branch serving four or more water closets where the branch is connected to a **stack** that receives any soil or waste from above. The relief vent shall connect to the circuit vented branch between the stack and the next upstream connected fixture drain to the circuit vented horizontal branch. The relief vent may be a dry vent or be a fixture branch or fixture drain for fixtures connected to the circuit vented horizontal branch with a maximum discharge of 4 drainage fixture units (dfu). For example if the circuit vented branch has a fixture drain serving a lavatory or a fixture branch serving back to back urinals or lavatories this pipe would work for the relief vent as well as long as the total dfu of the fixtures connected does not exceed 4 drainage fixture units (dfu).

914.3 of the Code. "The slope of the vent section of the horizontal branch drain shall be not greater than one unit in 12 units horizontal (8.3 percent). The entire length of the vent section of the horizontal branch drain shall be sized for the total drainage discharge to the branch". This means the slope cannot exceed 1 inch per foot and the circuit vent must remain the largest size required by the total discharge in drainage fixtures units throughout the entire circuit vented branch. If the dfu load from Table 710.1(2) requires a 4-inch pipe then 4 inch is the size of the entire circuit vented branch.

Sizing a Circuit Vented Branch. Determine the total drainage fixture units (dfu) discharged into the stack from Table 709.1. Then size the circuit vented branch based on Table 710.1(2). If the total dfu requires a 4-inch pipe then that size must be provided for the entire branch that serves all of the circuit vented connected fixture drains.

Sizing the dry vent. The dry vent serving the horizontal circuit vented branch shall be not less than ½ of the required drain size. If the drain is required to be 4 inch then the dry vent serving the branch shall not be less than 2 inch.

Because a circuit vented branch cannot exceed the 1 inch per foot slope, no vertical offsets are permitted in the branch and all circuit vented fixtures shall connect horizontally to the branch. Any additional fixtures in the bathroom are permitted to connect to the circuit vented branch as long as they are individually or common vented. An example would be lavatories or urinals in the same bathroom connected into the circuited vented branch through a vertical fixture drain or fixture branch.

CORRECT:
CIRCUIT VENT IS SLOPED A MAXIMUM
OF 1" PER FOOT. VERTICAL OFFSETS
ARE NOT PERMITTED ON THE CIRCUIT
VENT OR ITS FIXTURE DRAINS. ALL
FIXTURE DRAINS MUST CONNECT
HORIZONTAL TO THE CIRCUIT VENT.

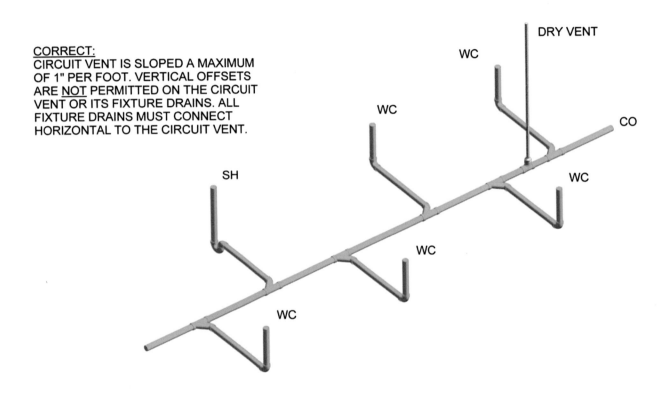

DRY VENT

WC

WC

CO

SH

WC

WC

WC

WC

DIAGRAM 133

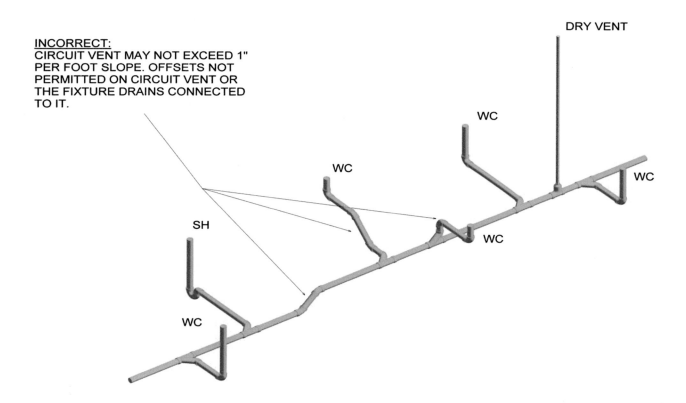

DRY VENT

INCORRECT:
CIRCUIT VENT MAY NOT EXCEED 1"
PER FOOT SLOPE. OFFSETS NOT
PERMITTED ON CIRCUIT VENT OR
THE FIXTURE DRAINS CONNECTED
TO IT.

WC

WC

SH

WC

WC

WC

DIAGRAM 134

DIAGRAM 135 A relief vent is required when a circuit vented branch has 4 or more water closets and is connected to a stack receiving discharge from horizontal branches from above. Notice the relief vent positioned between the stack and the first set of fixtures connected.

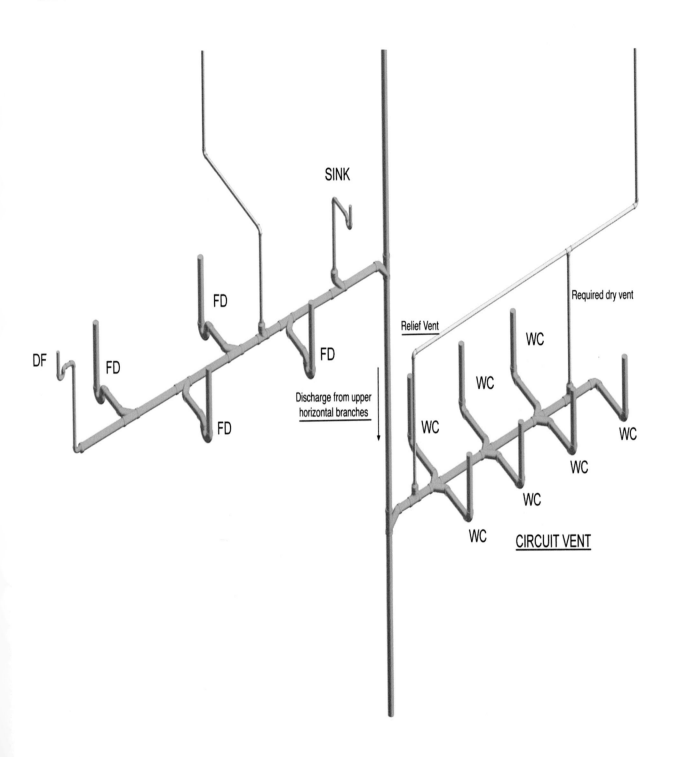

DIAGRAM 135

Diagram 136 A sized circuit vent. The circuit vented branch is sized to the total dfu discharged into the branch determined from Table 709.1 and 710.1(2) and remains full size throughout the circuit vented branch. The relief vent shall be sized to ½ of the required drain size. The dry vent serving the circuit vent is also sized to ½ of the required drain size. If the vent exceeds 40 feet in total developed length, then the vent must be increased by one pipe size for the entire developed length.

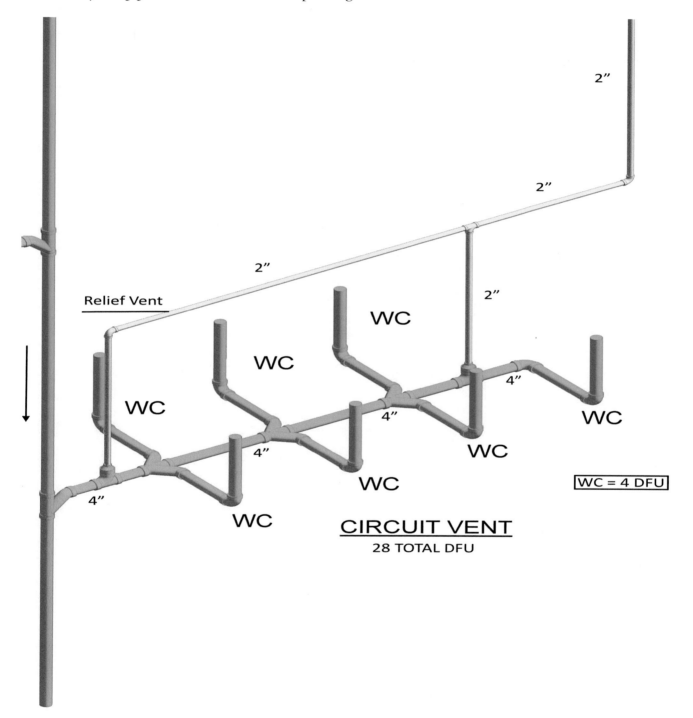

Diagram 136

Photograph 40 Circuit vents do not have to be large in size as seen below with only two water closets that are circuit vented. Anywhere from two to eight fixtures may be circuit vented.

Photograph 40

Photograph 41 Another small circuit vent picking up 3 fixtures. Notice the circuit vented branch remains full size throughout based on the largest pipe required for the total drainage fixture load.

Photograph 41

Photograph 42 The <u>dry vent</u> cannot receive the discharge of any fixtures and serves only as a vent.

Photograph 42

Photograph 43 Circuit vent with additional fixtures that are individually and common vented.

Photograph 43

Photograph 44 A large circuit vent with a relief vent. This circuit vent has 4 or more water closets and is connected to a stack receiving discharge from horizontal branches above.

Photograph 44

Photograph 45 There are two (multiple circuit vented branches) below. In the larger circuit vented branch below you can see another example of where to use a "double pattern" fitting. The Code states that the circuit dry vent be located between the two upper most circuit vented fixtures but as you can see in this example, it is also acceptable to use a double pattern fitting for the uppermost two fixtures with the dry vent located immediately downstream.

Photograph 45

Photograph 46 A circuit vented commercial carrier group of water closets.

Photograph 46

Photograph 47 The circuit vented branch remains full size throughout the circuit branch based on the total drainage fixture units discharged through it. The individually vented lavatories are connected to the branch and can be sized for the drainage fixture unit load of the lavatories only.

Photograph 47

7 WASTE STACK VENTING

913 of the Code. Waste Stack Venting is a very simple method to vent floor-to-floor fixtures. As with the other wet venting methods in this book, the pipe (stack) serves as the waste *and* the vent. The Waste Stack Vent shall not receive the discharge of water closets or urinals.

The Waste Stack Vent shall remain vertical. No offsets are permitted between the lowest fixture connection and the uppermost fixture drain connection. Offsets are permitted below the first fixture drain connection or at a minimum of 6 inches above the flood rim of the highest fixture drain connection.

Only *fixture drains* may connect to the stack. This means that individual fixtures are connecting to the stack and shall connect separately through an approved fitting such as a double Santee or double fixture fitting. Horizontal branches or fixture branches may not connect to the stack.

The Stack is sized on the total drainage fixture units discharged into the stack. The Stack shall remain undiminished in size throughout. The stack vent serving the waste stack shall be the same size as the stack and may connect to other vent stacks or stack vents in accordance with section 904.5 of the Code (Vent Headers).

TABLE 913.4
WASTE STACK SIZE

STACK SIZE (inches)	Maximum number of drainage fixture units (dfu)	
	Total discharge into one branch interval	Total discharge for stack
1 1/2	1	2
2	2	4
2 1/2	No limit	8
3	No limit	24
4	No limit	50
5	No limit	75
6	No limit	100

When sizing the Waste Stack Vent, calculate the drainage fixture units (dfu) of all of the fixtures connected to the stack. If you have a 1 ½" or a 2" stack notice that there are limits on each floor (branch interval). For example an 1 ½" stack could only receive 1 total dfu on each branch interval. This could be two drinking fountains at ½ dfu each picking up two floors (branch intervals). For a 2 " stack it could be two lavatories on each floor for a 2 story stack.

Photograph 48 In the commercial building below the installer used waste stack venting to pick up multiple floors of lavatories. The fixture drains connect separately through a Double Santee. The stack is 3 inch and will remain that size until it terminates.

Photograph 48

DIAGRAM 137 In the waste stack vent illustrated below only "fixture drains" or single fixtures are connecting to the stack and connect separately through an approved fitting. No offsets are permitted between the uppermost and the lowest fixture drain connections. The stack vent serving shall remain not less than the required stack size from Table 913.4. The waste stack is sized on the total discharge into the stack in accordance with Table 913.4.

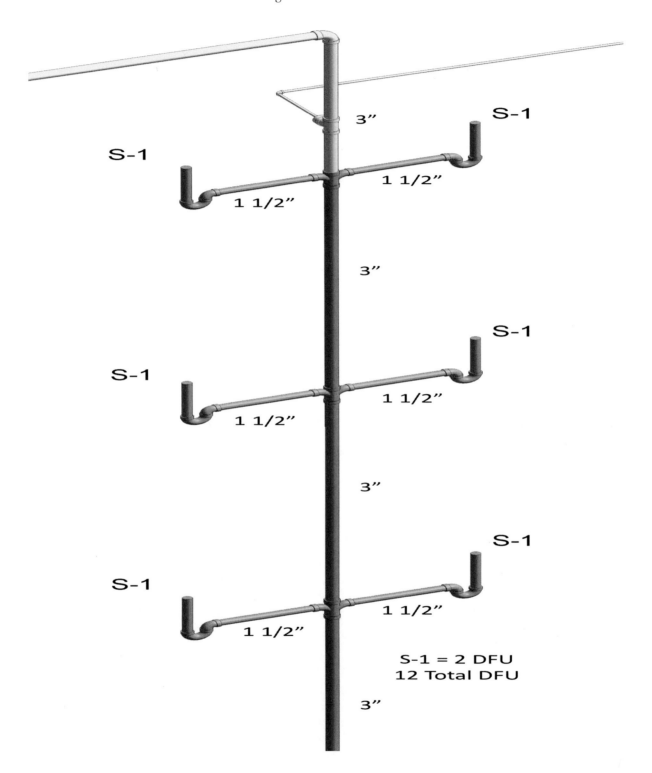

DIAGRAM 137
WASTE STACK VENTING

8 SINGLE STACK VENTING

Section 917 of the Code. New in the 2012 edition of the IPC, this system is similar to the Philadelphia Single Stack systems that have been in place in Pennsylvania for over a century. In contrast to the Waste Stack Vent this system allows horizontal branches to connect and allows all fixtures including water closets and urinals. The stack and the branches serve as both the vent and the drain when the stack is sized to Table 917.2 and the branches to Table 710.1(2).

There are of course specific rules that must be followed in order to install a Single Stack Vent system correctly. This system, like the Waste Stack Vent system shall remain full size throughout and the stack vent serving shall remain undiminished to termination.

Sizing the Stack. Use Table 917.2 to size the stack on the total drainage fixtures units (dfu) discharged into the stack.

TABLE 917.2
SINGLE STACK SIZE

Maximum Connected Drainage Fixture Units

STACK SIZE (inches)	Stacks less than 75 feet in height	Stacks 75 feet to less than 160 feet in height	Stacks 160 feet And greater in height
3	24	NP	NP
4	225	24	NP
5	480	225	24
6	1015	480	225
8	2320	1015	480
10	4500	2320	1015
12	8100	4500	2320
15	13600	8100	4500

* 3 inch Stacks shall not receive the discharge of more than two water closets.

Sizing the horizontal branches. Size the branches based on Table 710.1(2)

Water Closet Connections:
- Only one water closet may connect to a 3-inch horizontal branch within 18 horizontal inches of the stack.
- If a water closet connects within 18 inches measured horizontally from the stack and only one fixture with a drain size of 1 ½" connects to the same 3 inch branch. The branch connection to the stack shall be made with a sanitary tee. If the branch connection is made with a wye, only the water closet may discharge into the branch.
- The connection of a water closet to a horizontal branch shall not be more than 4 feet measured horizontally from the stack. Except that if the horizontal branch connects to the stack through a sanitary tee then the distance may be 8 feet.

Fixtures other than water closets: Fixture connections shall not be more than 12 feet measured horizontally from the stack. Any vertical piping of a fixture drain shall not be considered when determining stack to fixture distances.

Vertical piping. The minimum size diameter of any vertical piping of a fixture drain connecting to the horizontal branch is 2 inches. Water supplied urinals and standpipes vertical piping shall not be less than 3 inches in diameter. Fixture drains shall not exceed 4 feet in vertical height from the horizontal branch. If a fixture drain must exceed the vertical distance of 4 feet then is shall be increased in size or be individually vented.

Building Drains and sewers sizing. Building drains and sewers receiving the discharge from a single stack vent shall be sized based on the total drainage fixture load determined from Table 710.1(2).

Section 917.6 of the Code. An **additional vent** is required in the horizontal branch connecting to a single stack vent system if:

- There is a horizontal branch 4 inches or larger in diameter connected to the single stack vent system with two or more water closets.
- There is a horizontal branch connected through a wye that exceeds 4 feet in developed length from the stack to a water closet.
- There is a horizontal branch connected through a sanitary tee that exceeds 8 feet in developed length from the stack to a water closet.
- There is a fixture other than a water closet that connects more than 12 feet in developed length from the stack to the fixture trap.

The additional vent may be provided by individual vents, common vents, circuit vents, combination waste and vent or wet vents. The dry vent serving the additional vent shall terminate to a branch vent, vent stack, stack vent, air admittance valve or to the outdoors.

The allowance by Section 917.6 of the Code to incorporate other venting methods of Chapter 9 would also allow the venting systems used for additional venting to serve as the venting method for an entire branch connected to the single stack system. In other words, you may have horizontal branches connecting to the single stack system that conform to section 917 for single stack venting and you may also have other branches that are partially single stack and partial circuit vent or partial wet vent....or you may have a branch that is entirely circuit vented. It would not affect the function of the single stack with any combination of the venting systems listed above. **See Diagram 146.**

Section 917.7 Vertical offsets are allowed in a single stack system without any special additional venting. A vertical offset would be up to a 45-degree angle from the vertical. When it comes to **horizontal offsets** (greater than 45 degrees from the vertical) in the single stack system, there are a few rules to follow.

A vent must be provided for any horizontal offset where there are fixture drains or horizontal branches that connect to the single stack vent system *below* the offset. The vent shall be installed to **Section 907 of the Code** (vents for stack offsets). Also, no fixture drains or horizontal branches can connect to within 2 feet above or below the offset.

Section 917.8 This section prohibits any horizontal branches on the lower 2 floors of any single stack system serving a building with 3 or more floors and also prohibits any connections downstream of at least 10 pipe diameters of the base of the single stack.

DIAGRAM 138 A single stack with sizing. Note that not more than 2 water closets may discharge into a 3-inch stack.

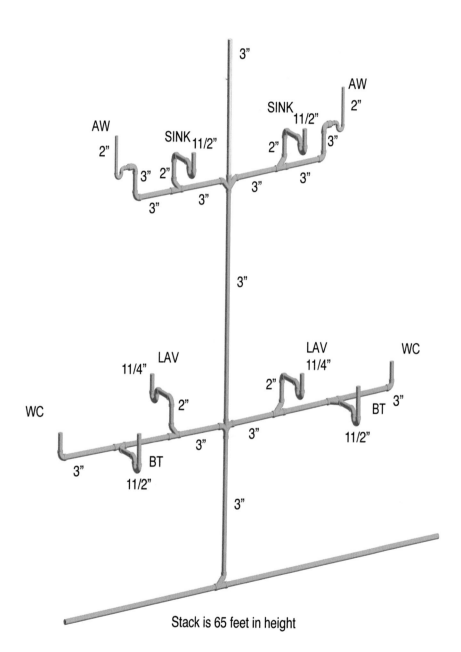

Bathroom group = 5 dfu

AW = 2dfu
Sink = 2dfu
Lav = 1dfu
BT = 2dfu

Stack is 65 feet in height

DIAGRAM 138

DIAGRAM 139 Single stack fixtures other than water closets are limited to 12 feet measured horizontally from the stack. Water closets connected to the stack with a sanitary tee may not exceed 8 feet. Water closets connected to the stack with a wye may not exceed 4 feet. Only two water closets permitted on a 3-inch stack. A 3-inch stack may not exceed 75 feet in height or carry more than 24 dfu. The stack vent remains the same size as the stack to termination.

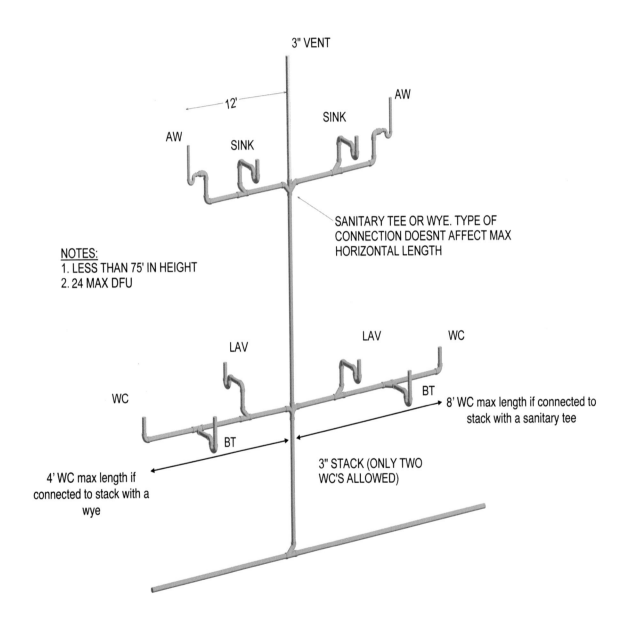

DIAGRAM 139

DIAGRAM 140 2 inch is the minimum size for any vertical piping serving a fixture drain. The vertical fixture drain may not exceed 4 feet. Water supplied urinals and standpipes require a 3-inch minimum vertical fixture drain.

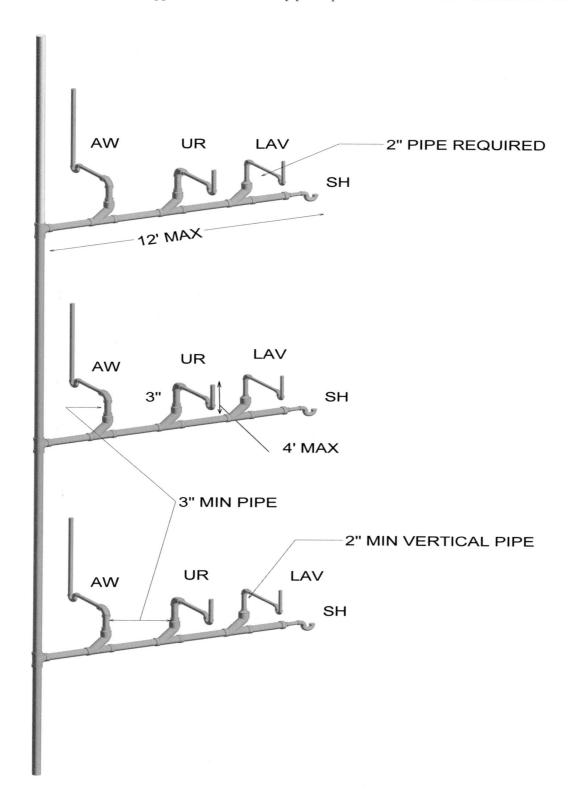

DIAGRAM 140

DIAGRAM 141 The chart below illustrates the maximum developed length from the stack to the fixture trap as measured horizontally from the stack. Note that the type of connection to the stack affects the water closet lengths but not other fixtures. The use of a sanitary tee in lieu of a wye can double the allowable distance for water closets.

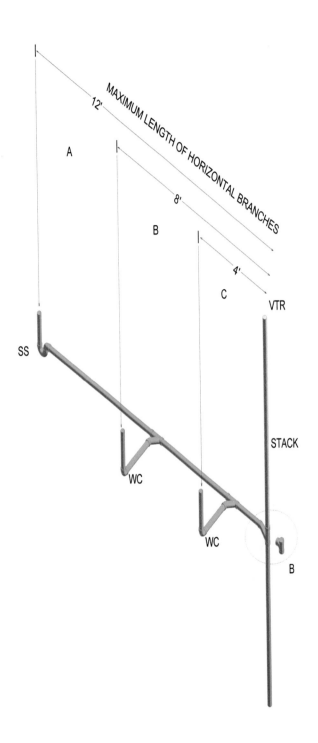

NOTES:

A. FIXTURES OTHER THAN WATER CLOSETS TYPE OF CONNECTION TO STACK IS IRRELEVANT.

B. WATER CLOSET ON A BRANCH CONNECTED TO STACK BY A SANITARY TEE.

C. WATER CLOSET CONNECTED TO STACK BY A WYE FITTING

DIAGRAM 141

DIAGRAM 142 Only one water closet may connect to a 3-inch branch within 18 inches of the stack. If a water closet connects to a 3-inch branch that is connected to the stack by a wye fitting and is within 18 inches of the stack, the water closet is the only fixture permitted on the branch. Notice that no fixtures or branches are permitted to connect to the single stack on the lower two floors.

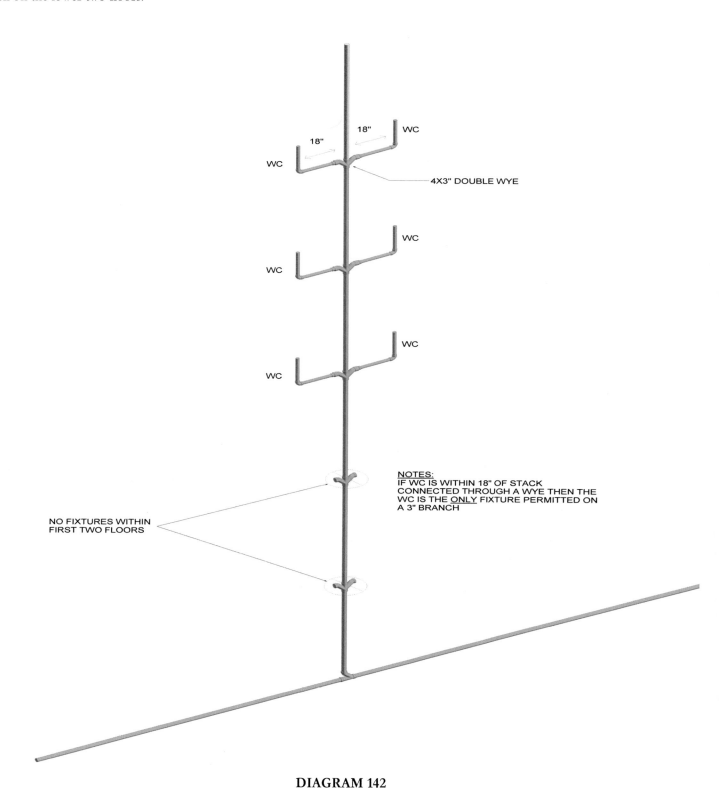

DIAGRAM 142

DIAGRAM 143 A sized single stack. Horizontal branches are sized to Table 709.1 and 710.1(2). All four branches are the same. Kitchen Sink = 2dfu, Bathroom Group = 5dfu. Total dfu per branch = 7dfu. Total dfu for the stack = 28. Based on the column for stacks less than 75 feet in height the stack size is 4 inch.

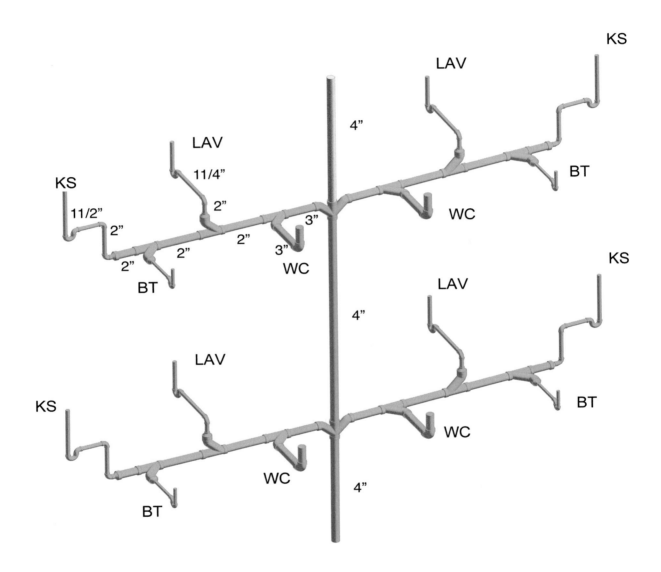

STACK LESS THAN 75 FEET IN HEIGHT

DIAGRAM 143

DIAGRAM 144 Upper branch B: Additional venting is required on a branch with two or more water closets. The additional venting was achieved by using a horizontal wet vent. Lower branch A: The horizontal measured developed length exceeded the 12 feet permitted so additional venting was achieved by using a common vent.

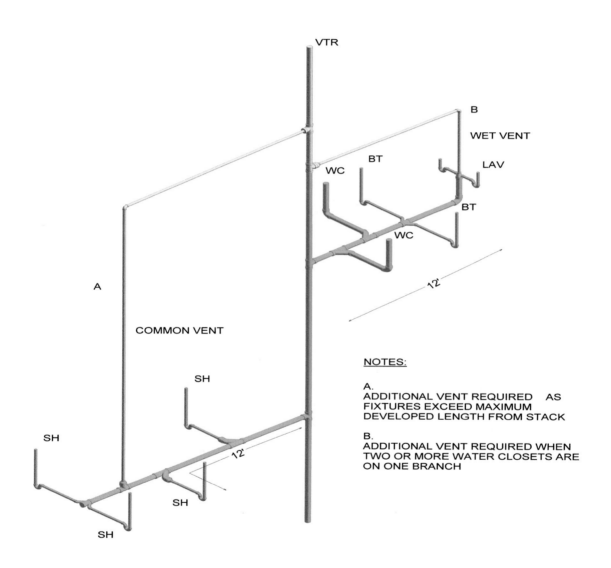

NOTES:

A.
ADDITIONAL VENT REQUIRED   AS
FIXTURES EXCEED MAXIMUM
DEVELOPED LENGTH FROM STACK

B.
ADDITIONAL VENT REQUIRED WHEN
TWO OR MORE WATER CLOSETS ARE
ON ONE BRANCH

DIAGRAM 144

DIAGRAM 145 The additional venting here was required because there are fixtures beyond the 12-foot limit. The additional venting was achieved with a circuit vented branch. The relief vent is provided since the branch serves 4 or more water closets and there is discharge from upper horizontal branches.

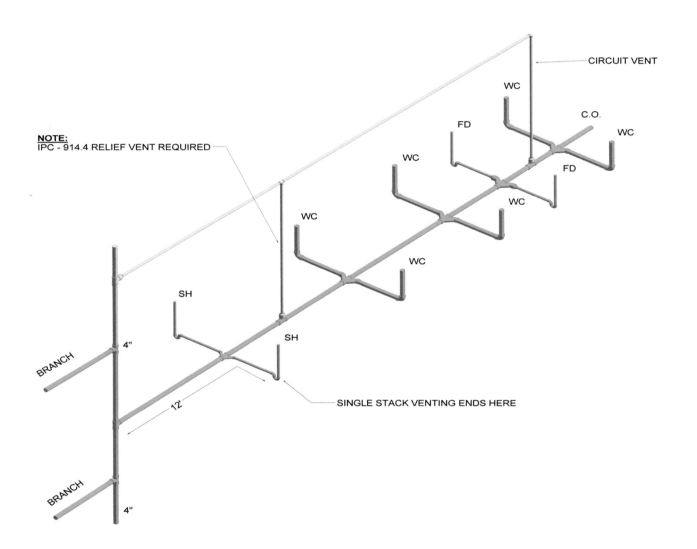

DIAGRAM 145

DIAGRAM 146A This 7 branch interval single stack shows most of the floors meeting the rules of single stack to fixture horizontal distances. The upper two floors require additional venting. Notice the lower two floors are picked up on a separate stack.

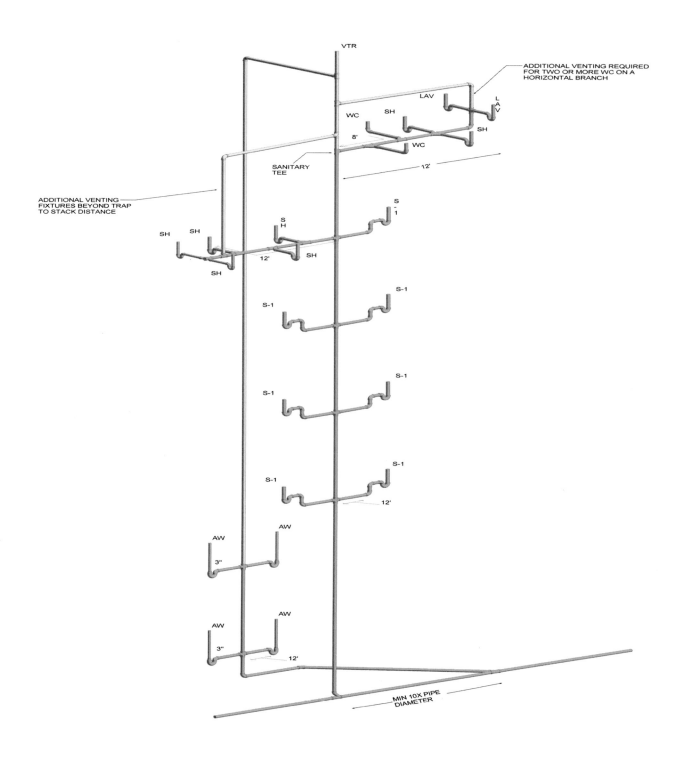

DIAGRAM 146A

DIAGRAM 146B A closer look at the upper two floors of **DIAGRAM 146A.**

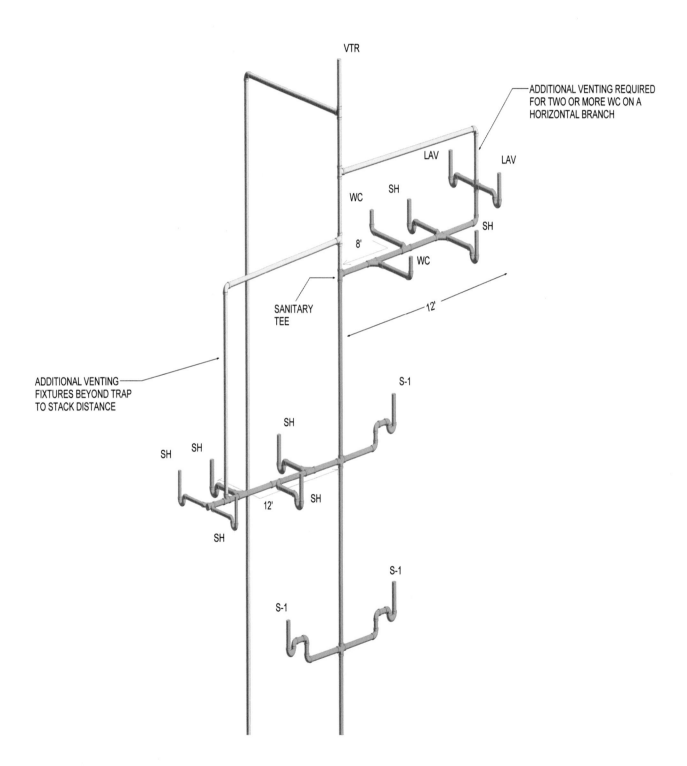

DIAGRAM 146B

DIAGRAM 147 No fixtures or branches can connect to the lower two floors of a single stack. The lower two floors may connect to a separate stack as shown below. The separate stack shall connect no less than 10 pipe diameters downstream of the base of the single stack.

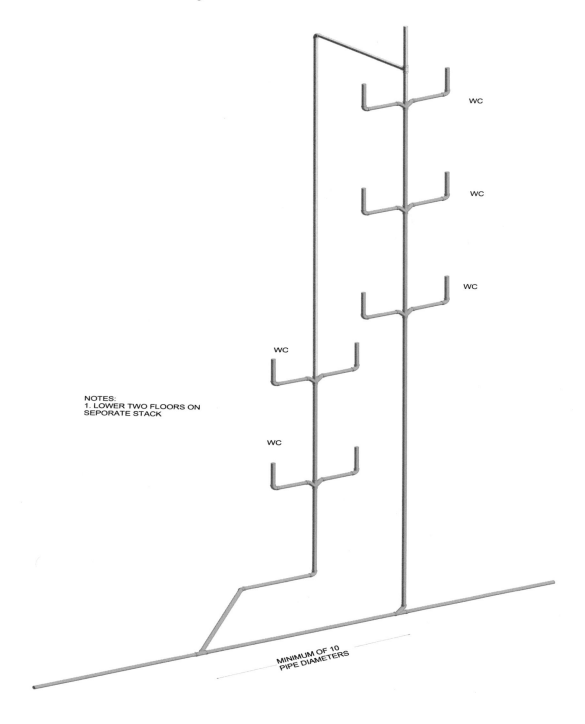

DIAGRAM 147

DIAGRAM 148 A single stack with other properly vented branches connected.

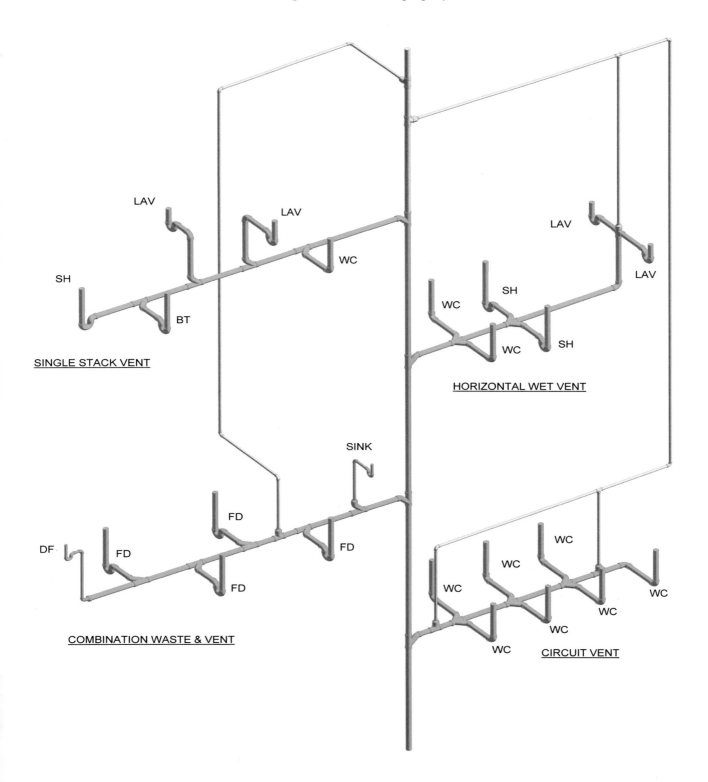

DIAGRAM 148

9 AIR ADMITTANCE VALVES (AAV'S)

Section 918 of the Code. AAV's can be installed many times when conventional venting just won't work. Whether due to structural conditions or for saving labor and materials, an AAV may be the right choice for a venting termination. These can be used for individual vents, branch vents, circuit vents and stack vents. Be sure to use the right AAV for the right application. Individual and branch type AAVs are listed to ASSE 1051. Stack type AAVs are listed to ASSE 1050. If the AAV is being used in a chemical waste system it shall be listed to ASSE 1049.

When used for individual, branch or circuit venting the AAV shall be listed to ASSE 1051. There are similar type valves out there that are not tested to this standard and would not be accepted by code. Individual and branch type AAV's shall be located on the same floor as the fixtures they are venting and shall connect to a horizontal branch.

Relief vents A relief vent is required when using an AAV on multi story buildings and the horizontal branch you are venting with the AAV is located more than 4 branch intervals from the top of the stack. The relief vent shall connect to the horizontal branch between the most downstream fixture and the stack. The connection must follow the rules of the other vents covered in this manual in that the use of the correct fittings whether it is a dry vent, a Santee on its back or a Combo on its back whether the relief vent is solely dry or serving as a fixture drain (if the relief vent is venting a fixture). The relief vent shall rise to 6 inches above the flood rim of the highest fixture served before offsetting or combining with other vents and shall either terminate at a vent stack, stack vent or extend to the outdoors. The relief vent is sized at ½ of the diameter of the required drain size of the horizontal branch.

Stack type AAVs. Stack type AAVs shall be listed to ASSE 1050. These can be used for the vent terminal for vent stacks or stack vents as long as the stack that the vent is serving does not exceed 6 branch intervals.

Installation The basic rules for installing AAV's:

- Shall be located a minimum of 4 inches above the horizontal branch or fixture drain being vented.
- "Stack type" shall be located a minimum of 6 inches above the flood rim of the highest fixture served.
- Shall be located a minimum of 6 inches above any insulation.
- Location shall not exceed the developed length permitted for the vent.
- Shall have access and ventilation. Access to remove and repair the valve and airflow to operate.
- At least one vent must extend to the outdoors on any system with an AAV installed.
- Shall not be located in supply or return air plenums.
- Shall not be used on sumps or ejectors without an engineered design.

Installers and inspectors should familiarize themselves with the manufacturer's installation requirements as well as the Code. In instances where the manufacturer and the Code conflict, the more restrictive provision shall apply. **(Section 301.7 of the Code).**

DIAGRAM 149 The AAV shall be located a minimum of 4 inches above the horizontal branch.

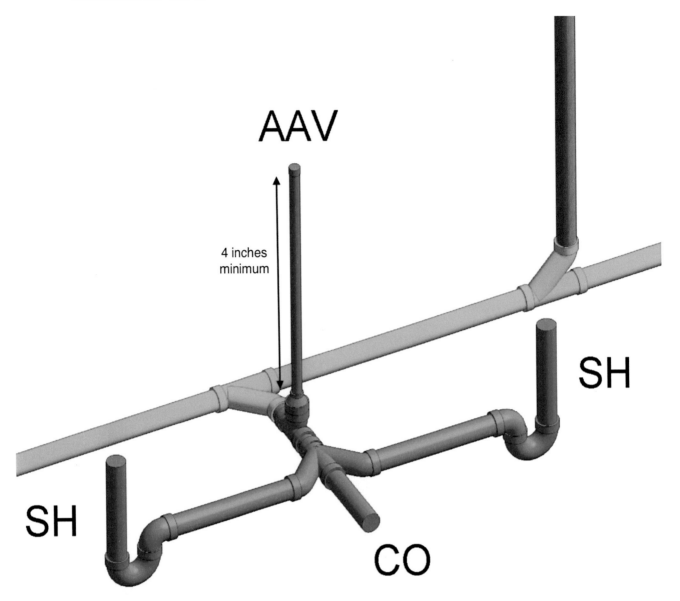

DIAGRAM 149

Photograph 49 This commercial installation shows an AAV box located well above the fixture. The box will have a removable grill, which will allow access and ventilation. This AAV would be an individual vent listed to ASSE 1051.

Photograph 49

Photograph 50 AAV installed on a PVC vent.

Photograph 50

Photograph 51 AAV box with grill installed.

Photograph 51

Section 916 of the Code. Island venting is only for sinks or lavatories. This method may be used in situations where you may have a sink located under a window or structural beam or other obstruction that does not allow a traditional vent. Many times an installer will opt for an AAV in these cases or maybe even a combination waste and vent. But if the sink has a food waste disposer then the combo waste and vent is not an option. Some people just don't want the worry of a mechanical failure on an AAV (AAVs have rigorous testing and are safe and reliable) but anything mechanical can fail. If either of the above are the case, then island fixture venting may be the solution.

DIAGRAM 149 shows an example of a properly installed island fixture. The horizontal vent shall be sloped back towards the fixture and sized at a minimum of ½ of the required drain size. Cleanouts must be provided for cleaning in all directions of the island vent.

ISLAND FIXTURE VENTING

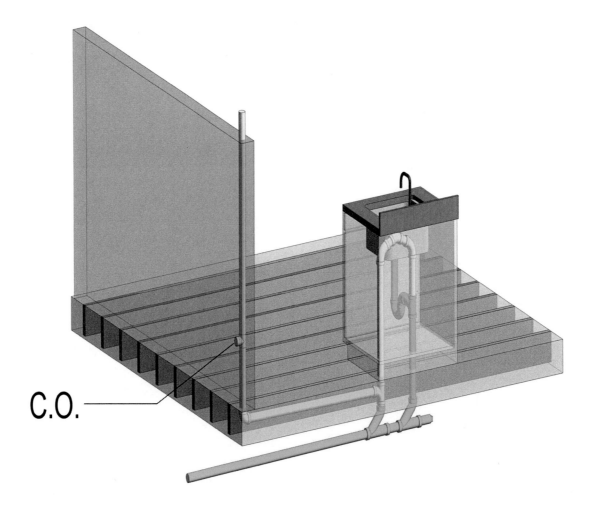

C.O.

DIAGRAM 150

DIAGRAM 151 Identify the four different venting systems below. A, B, C and D

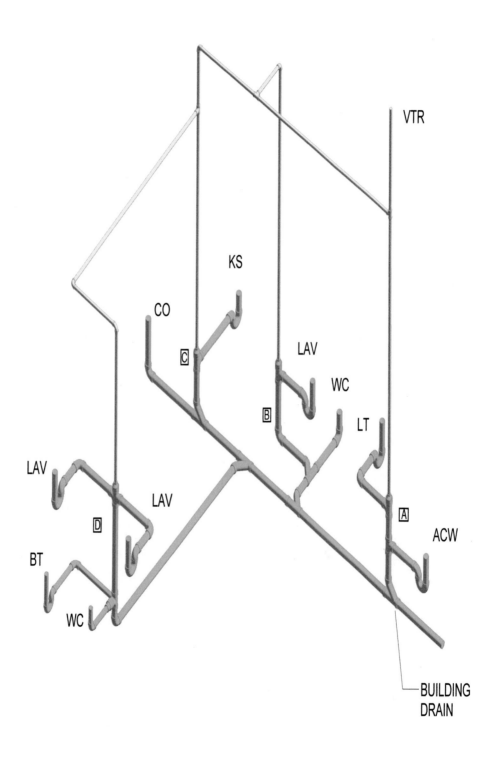

DIAGRAM 151

DIAGRAM 152 Identify the seven different venting systems below. A, B, C, D, E, F & G

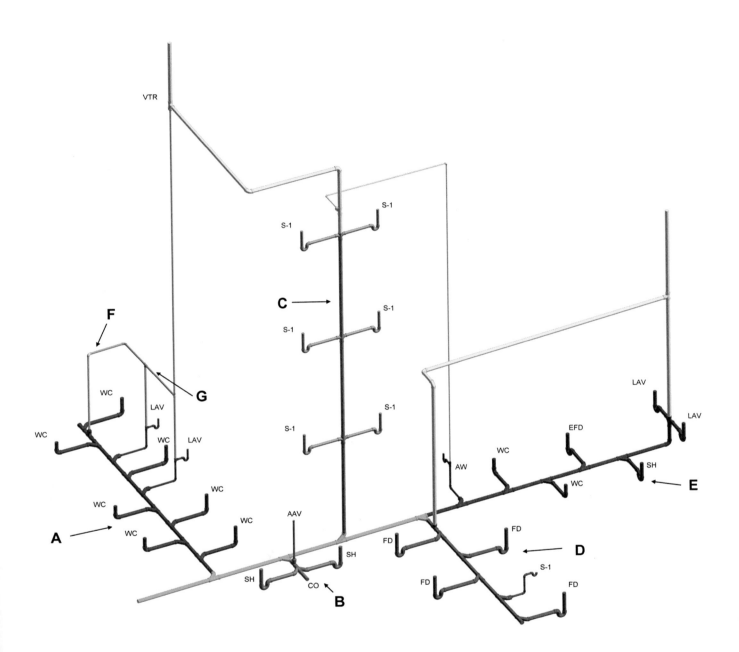

DIAGRAM 152

DIAGRAM 151 Answers:

A = Common Vent connections at different levels

B = Horizontal Wet Vent

C = Individual Vent

D = Vertical Wet Vent

DIAGRAM 152 Answers:

A = Circuit Vent

B = Common Vent

C = Waste Stack Vent

D = Combination Waste and Vent

E = Horizontal Wet Vent

F = Individual Vent

G = Branch Vent

AMAZON.COM

Made in the USA
San Bernardino, CA
17 July 2019